WINNING YOUR WORLD

GILES STEVENS

Copyright © 2013 by Giles Stevens

All Rights Reserved

Email: admin@vinechurch.co.uk
Web: www.vinechurch.co.uk

    Edition: Alice Goodwin-Hudson
    Cover Artwork: Sam Gretton
    Layout: John Lewis

Contents

5   Introduction: **PRODUCTIVITY** Principles

8   **PRICE** Principles
      Everything in the Kingdom of God has a price.
      Only those in credit can help those in debit.
      The prize is worth the price.

19   **PRAYER** Principles
      Human intercession leads to divine intervention.
      Pray and you'll be led, don't pray and you'll be driven.
      Divine intimacy determines public ministry.

28   **PRIORITY** Principles
      Make God's priority your priority.
      If you don't do the most important things first, you never get them done at all.
      You will either live by priorities or by pressures.

37   **PERSPECTIVE** Principles
      If you can see the bigger picture, you will act in a bigger way.
      A proper perspective is to see as God sees.
      Your obstacles are your opportunities.

46   **PREPARATION** Principles
      When opportunity meets preparation you find God's favour.
      It is better to look ahead and prepare than look back and regret.
      Great communicators make profound things simple to understand.

57 **PARTNERSHIP** Principles
    Teamwork makes the dream work.
    Every member is a minister.
    If you know the way you must show the way.

67 **PROVISION** Principles
    Every believer must input their time.
    Every believer must involve their talents.
    Every believer must invest their treasures.

78 **PASSION** Principles
    Victory comes to the passionate.
    Vision is the catalyst of passion.
    Passion attracts.

90 **PERSISTENCE** Principles
    Persistence breaks down resistance.
    Champions do what needs to be done
        even when they don't feel like it.
    Everybody takes knocks, but champions
        are the ones who get up quickly.

97 **PENTECOST** Principles
    You are empowered through a personal Pentecost.
    Your function is to flow in God's unction.
    You can only give what you have received.

108 **CONCLUSION:** Principles in Action

109 **APPENDIX:** Information about The 11th Question Project

Preface

I have added the subtitle to the English version "How to be fruitful in barren land" due to the current spiritual and religious climate in Europe. My ministry to date has been split quite evenly between working in the developed nations of Europe and developing nations of Asia and South America. Over recent years I have invested a lot of time in Brazil where we have been seeing our churches growing wonderfully. Peter Wagner once described Revival as church growth above 10% per annum. If this is the case, then we really have been experiencing revival as many of our smaller churches are seeing high percentage growth and even the large ones are maintaining 30% per year – which is a lot of people if you have a church of hundreds or thousands. Much of what we have seen there is similar to what I believe happened in Europe in times of the Reformation – the protestant message of salvation by faith is spreading like wild-fire, the emphasis on a personal encounter with the living God, the use of the Bible by the masses to build a personal relationship with the Lord rather than depend upon the clerics.

But what about Europe and the Post-modern West in our times? Is there hope for our churches here? Can the glory days of the past become a reality again? Can God revive His work here in the midst of our years, as the ancient prophet Malachi cried?

Whilst we know that the church has traditionally grown fastest in poorer and more needy nations, we should not use this as an excuse for failure. The environment may be different but we believe that God's principles and power remain the same. Hence if we use them the results will be there. Added to this it is a deception to look at our western communities and decide whether it can be saved or not. Too often I have heard the argument "It may work there but it won't work here". Why not? I wonder. "People are not interested here", they say. But wait a minute, I think. Since when do the unbelievers determine whether God will move in their families, cities or nations? No, no, no! Let us think correctly here. This is our job. This is the churches' responsibility. As goes the church, so goes the world. We are the ones who determine the future of our cities. If we pay the price and practice the principles, the future will be glorious. Does not our Lord watch over His word to perform it?

God's blessing is upon those who are dedicated to his purposes.

We cannot expect God to bless that which he has not ordained. His blessing is in line with his purposes. Too often we devise plans then ask the Lord to bless them, rather than seek the plans of the Lord, which, if we discover and deliver, will have his blessing upon them.

In Genesis 1.28 we read that the Lord blessed Adam and Eve and said to them; Be fruitful, multiply and fill the earth. The blessing comes with instruction or for a purpose. Jesus said it succinctly: The Spirit of the Lord is upon me, He has anointed me, to preach the Gospel to the poor.

In other words, by doing His will we will see his wonder. By obeying His leading, we will never be in need. Catch His vision and you get His provision. Or even, where He guides, He provides.

This all sounds good to us until He leads us to a place that we consider to be a disaster zone, a missionary's mortuary, a valley of dry bones. Yet, as Ezekiel teaches us, the Lord only does this to show us that in reality His kingdom is only build by supernatural power. It is in places of death that God chooses to reveal His life – upon the dry, waterless, plantless, lifeless mountain of Sinai, God meet Moses and released a river of living water; in Golgotha gaping graves, the King of Glory sprung to life.

I believe that the Lord would have a conversation with us similar to the one He had with Ezekiel thousands of years ago:
"Can these dry bones live?" He would ask again today.
"Oh Lord, you know." We should reply. "You know they can. With You all things are possible."
And He would respond again today: "Then prophesy to these bones and let my heavenly wind blow life into them again as it did first when I kissed

Adam."

Our work is a supernatural one indeed. Miraculous power is the prerequisite for any type of success. Without it, we labour in vain. With it, God reveals the glory of Christ and we are left simply boasting in our weaknesses rather than our strengths.

Miraculous power, we discover, is on offer. But only if we are fulfilling His purpose. It is the obedient that eat the good of the land (see Deut 28).

In Genesis 26 we read the extraordinary account of God's blessing upon Isaac, son of Abraham, when a terrible famine ravaged the land. Isaac was tempted to flee to Egypt to seek relief. At this time, Egypt was the centre of civilization, the prosperous and well-ordered nation of the day, the superpower. I have seen in all my own missionary travels how many people from developing nations want to come and live in the United States or even Western Europe. They understandably want to better their lives and believe they can better prosper and be better protected in these nations. All this makes sense to the natural mind. But what do you do if God gives you specific instructions not to leave, but rather to stay put? And further still to invest the little you do have in your own barren land. This was the challenge before Isaac. The Lord said to him; "Go not down into Egypt but dwell in the land that I shall tell thee of."

Now we have a problem. It makes good sense to leave; after all, other sensible people are leaving. But "there is a way that seems right to man and its end is the way of death" (Pr 4.6). We are challenged at times like this, to lean not unto our own understanding. As we thereby act in faith (for we are not walking by sight or our senses now but rather by the word of God), we suddenly find another power at work on our behalf. The supernatural blessing of the Lord begins to manifest. We read in verse 12: "Then Isaac sowed in that land and received in the same year an hundredfold; and the Lord blessed him and the man waxed great, and went forward, and great until he became very great." Whilst other peoples' fortunes were being reversed, Isaac was pressing forward and prospering. The tables had turned.

I share this as a prophetic word to those of you here in the West. If we are called to build great churches here, then we will succeed, by the grace of God. We do not need to fly to Africa to see great results or experience God moving. It is ours for the taking. We shall be fruitful in barren land.

So here in the English version of Winning Your World are the ageless principles that have helped churches throughout the centuries and throughout the cultures to conquer their communities for Christ. "Try me and see", says the Lord, "if I will not pour out such a blessing that you will not have room to contain it" (Mal 3.10). Come, and let's put these principles to practice.

Introduction
PRODUCTIVITY Principles

A renowned evangelist was talking to a friend and sharing his vision of winning the nations for Christ. On hearing the magnitude of his plans, the friend exclaimed; "Do you really think your ministry can win the whole world for Christ?" The evangelist replied; "No! …but we are going to try."

I converted to Christ in Melbourne, Australia, in 1992 when I was working there as a foreign businessman. Immediately I set about telling my friends and work colleagues the story of how my life had radically changed having met Jesus. On a long holiday back in my homeland, England, I met up with family members and old-school and university friends to tell them about the hope I had found in Christ. Those I could not get to meet personally I wrote to or telephoned. This was the start of my "evangelistic" journey. Like many who have gone before me I had joined the army of "witnesses" to tell the story of God's way to win back the world.

This journey led me to the mission fields of Asia for three years and then back to London, England where I worked as a full time evangelist holding outreach meetings in many cities in Europe.

Having married my Brazilian wife in 2000, I resolved to come and work in South America for a season of life and was warmly received by a local church, named Videira, in the city of Goiania. Since then this has been our home. It was here that I had first hand experience of "every member ministry". Our evangelism is not left to a department or zealous selection of members. Rather, week in week out, all the members of the church work together towards the same goal. Our passion is for each of us to "father" spiritual children and then to train them to be mature men and women of God.

Similar to the renowned evangelist, our vision is to win our generation for Christ. (It is the only purpose worth living for and dying for.) The fact that there are those who refuse to convert does not deter us. We are going to press on hoping that millions do. We are not under an illusion that the whole world will convert in one huge end-time revival. For we know that the Anti-Christ will come (and its system is already at work) that will deceive great portions of every nation. We are not focused on building a Greater Britain or blessed Brazil but rather we are passionate about building a new holy nation, called the Church, which is made up of people from every tribe, nation and tongue. It is to this end we work and we believe that millions will flood into this family of believers in our generation.

We do not believe that this is the responsibility of the evangelist or the church leaders alone. Rather their principle work is to train and inspire each member of the church to fulfil their ministries (Eph 4:11-12). Our reasoning is both scriptural and logical. Which strategy will save more people? For a minister to hold an evangelistic event for thousands? Or for that minister to train thousands of others to evangelise as a life-style? The answer to this question led me to dedicate much of my ministry to training others to do the work of the ministry. It is not that I am opposed to large evangelistic events. Of course not! Jesus held them and large crusades have had fantastic results. Therefore we value such strategies highly and hold them periodically. Nonetheless Jesus spent more time training his disciples than He did holding large scale events.

On a pure results basis, we have seen how the best form of evangelism is through each church member reaching out on a day to day basis into their already established networks of friends and colleagues at home and at work.

I have written this book for this reason – to put tools in the hands of every member of the church so that you can be successful in winning your sphere of influence for Jesus.

Some years ago when the Berlin Wall came down and Russia opened up for evangelism, many foreign preachers organised evangelistic events there. The underground church movement surfaced and we were much helped by the foreign preachers who came to hold campaigns. The same evangelist

I mentioned earlier also went to the former USSR. His events were highly attended, thousands were healed and saved, but in addition he spent much time training others for the work of evangelism. A comment by a local pastor has stuck in my mind on reflection of the evangelist's campaign. He said; "Brother, we have received a number of foreign ministers here recently and after their meetings we know that they are men of God! But after your meetings we now that we are men of God!"

This principle is at the heart this book. God is separating to Himself a people who are faithful, anointed, and full of passion for Him and His Kingdom. We are all called to be champions for Him; to overcome in His name. God is faithful to equip those whom He calls. He gives us the capacity for the task at hand.

Working with one heart, one mind, and one purpose, we have the potential of winning more people to Christ than any other period of history. Individually we may be weak but united we are a mighty force. A huge waterfall is made up of millions of tiny droplets flowing together. If you work to win your world and I work to win mine, we can be part of the greatest outpouring of God's Spirit that this world has ever seen!

PRICE Principles

"Bear up the hands that hang down, by faith and prayer; support the tottering knees. Have you any days of fasting and prayer? Storm the throne of grace and persevere therein, and mercy will come down."

John Wesley

1st PRICE Principle
Everything in the Kingdom of God has a price.

I asked church leaders in one of the churches where I worked why they think that the church is growing at such a rate, they may tell you about the favour of God on the work. But dig a little deeper and you will hear the leaders also talk about Blood, Sweat & Tears! – The blood of self-sacrifice, the tears of Intercession, and the sweat of hard work.

In the Kingdom of God everything has a price. You cannot obtain the blessings unless you pay the price. The world was created for mankind, not mankind for the world. People are the pinnacle and prize of God's creation. There is nothing more important and nothing more valuable. Yet to win them for Christ will cost us everything. We believe that if we want to reap souls, we must give our own soul. The question is; "Are we willing to pay such a price?" Or in other words, "Are we willing to die to self that others might live?"

"Most assuredly, I say to you, unless a grain of wheat falls into the ground and dies, it remains alone; but if it dies, it produces much grain." John 12:24

The biblical principle is simple – we will reap what we sow - in giving our own lives that we are able to win other lives. By sowing our own life, we reap the lives of others. Jesus was the seed of God who was planted in the ground, through His sacrificial death, and who rose again and now bears much fruit. He is the first born of many brethren. Biblical principles must be followed if we want to see biblical results.

God has limited Himself to only work through those who follow His principles. The life force of God is only at work in us, when we are dead to self. Yet unless we die to self, His life cannot be manifested in us. Those who simply talk the talk but don't walk the walk have little fruit to their names.

*The price we must consistently pay
is the death of self in order that others may live.*

We must also remember that the Satan, the god of this world, and his demonic cohorts, are serious contenders for the souls of mankind. They will not simply hand over their captives to the person who timidly taps at the prison door. Victory only comes to those who relentlessly storm their dark kingdom.

The book of Acts recounts the story of the seven sons of Sceva who tried in vain to caste out the demons from one man only to be overwhelmed, stripped, and beaten by this demon-possessed man. The demons cried; "Jesus we acknowledge, and Paul we know, but who are you?" (Acts 19:14-16). To be known in heaven is one thing but to be feared in hell is another. The demonic realm acknowledges the matchless name of Jesus but they release their prisoners only to those who, like the Apostle Paul, are filled with the life-force and presence of Christ. English evangelist Smith Wigglesworth said; "All of me, none of Christ; some of me, some of Christ; none of me, all of Christ". Indeed we must decrease if we want the Christ in us to increase.

Anything worth having is going to be a struggle

Each weekend in Goiania, Brazil we held a series of "Encounter with God" Camps every weekend. Normally we fill each of our 6 camps with up to 120 unbelievers. Our statistics show that whilst over 90% commit to Christ at the camp, approximately 30% go on to be baptised and join our church. Our teams fast and pray for the week prior to the camps and our cell groups are mobilised to spend the week inviting friends to come. Friday nights our church car park fills with people from all walks of life, waiting to be shipped out to one of the camps. The first night is spiritual struggle. Some don't want to listen to the message, some want to hang outside and smoke or take drugs, some want to go home, and others try to interrupt the preaching – it's a fight. But come Sunday morning the majority of them are wonderfully saved and filled with the Spirit.

Recently we held our largest ever encounter weekend, with nearly 6000 unbelievers packed into our two church buildings for 2 days of intense ministry. As we lifted our hands to praise the Lord in our opening worship song, I saw a number of people openly weeping, clearly touched by God's presence. We had not preached a word, we had not mentioned the presence of God's Spirit, but here He was in action almost before we had started. Why such quick and remarkable results? I believe it was because the price had already been paid for these precious souls (1,500 of them went on to be baptised the following day). For 40 days preceding the event, thousands of church members had fasted (either total or partial fasts) and prayed privately and corporately (at least twice a day). Yes the heavens had been wrenched; the battle had already been fought and won; now it was time to reap the harvest.

"Those who sow in tears shall reap in joy. He who continually goes forth weeping, bearing seed for sowing, shall doubtless come again with rejoicing, bringing his sheaves with him." (Ps 126:5-6)

I believe that when a Christian offers up his own life for the benefit of another, the whole of heaven is alerted. The children of Israel rebelled against God on many occasions on their exodus from Egypt. In Exodus chapter 32 we read how the Israelites made a golden calf and began to worship it, whilst Moses was on Mount Sinai. When he came down the mountain he was furious. He rebuked the people and ground the golden calf to powder. God's anger likewise burned against His people because of their rebelliousness. (Previously God had threatened to wipe them all out and start a completely new chosen family through Moses.) Yet Moses interceded for them in a manner that, I believe, would have surprised every angel in heaven.

"Oh, these people have committed a great sin, and have made for themselves a god of gold! Yet now, if You will forgive their sin – but if not, I pray, **blot me out of your book which you have written**". (Exodus 32:32 Emphasis mine).

Moses was not just putting his life on the line, but his eternity on the line. He was saying; "Lord, if you destroy them, then destroy me too! " A disregard of self for the sake of others has always alerted heaven and been met with huge out-pourings of God's power. I believe the trinity rejoice when they find people who are acting in such a godly sacrificial manner. No wonder he was able to save so many million people from certain judgement and death.

Likewise the Apostle Paul, no doubt well versed in these scriptures as they are part of the Jewish Torah, revealed the price he was willing to pay to see his own nation saved:

"I tell the truth in Christ, I am not lying, my conscience also bearing witness in the Holy Spirit, that I have great sorrow and continual grief in my heart. For I could wish that I myself were accursed from Christ for my brethren, my own countrymen according to my flesh." (Romans 9:1-2)

Small wonder that this man was such a prolific soul-winning and church-builder, even being accused of turning the world upside down.

"If Jesus Christ be God and died for me, then no sacrifice can be too great for me to make for Him."
C.T. Studd

But is this just pie-in-the-sky Christianity for average believers like you and me? Is this God's standard for all of us or just a few who are endowed with extraordinary portion of grace?

In Revelation 12:11 we read:

"And they (the believers) overcame him (the devil) by the blood of the lamb and by the word of their testimony, and they did not love their lives to the death."

Many believers know the first two phrases of this scripture but forget the last – that our victory is based upon not loving our lives to the death. The word "life" in this scripture is the same and the word "soul" in Greek. In other words - victory is dependant upon not loving our souls excessively. Hence the angel of heaven who spoke these words is instructing us to be spiritual and not soulful. It was not just a word to encourage martyrs in their hour of trial, but to encourage all of us to pay the price of spirituality – to not be led by the flesh, as immature people are, but rather to discipline our personal desires that we might be victorious in Christ and for Christ.

2ND PRICE PRINCIPLE
ONLY THOSE IN CREDIT CAN HELP THOSE IN DEBIT.

Due to our sins, we were all in debt to God. However, Jesus lived a sinless life and then took upon Himself the sins of the world. He was in credit and paid for those of us who were in debit. Therefore whilst we are thankful that salvation is a free gift, we must never forget that it was not free for God. It cost the Father the very blood of His only Son to redeem us.

Winning of our friends and families for Christ also comes at a price. Not-yet-believers are not able to intercede for their own salvation, they are dependant upon those who have access to the throne room of God and who have power over the realm of darkness. Every believer has been equipped to be a liberator of the captives. The anointing of God is upon us for this purpose (Luke 4:18).

Not-yet-believers are not able to pay the price; they have not credit with God. But sons have the right to use the father's supplies. Sons have credit because they are now part of God's family.

Whilst in each of our campaigns we delight to tell seekers that eternal life is for free, we know that for us their salvation has cost something. If we had not paid the price in prayer and fasting and hard work, they would probably not be sitting listening to us.

There are no magic formulas or secret strategies to winning souls. In our modern culture of wanting everything free and easy, few people seem disposed to walk this path of self-sacrifice. People want things now and they want them without sweat or strain. Most people have sold out for a life of warm comfort and trivial delights rather than a life of noble purpose and pursuit.

Tragically there are also those who, whilst priding themselves in being faithful husbands or in being committed tithers, pray little, fast rarely if at all, and give minimal effort toward winning their world for Christ.

> *Many people want the rewards of success without paying the price.*

Spiritually immature people have little control over their carnal desires. They may be full of good intentions, but few of them fulfil those intentions. As the saying goes "The road to hell is paved with intentions!"

"The flesh lusts against the Spirit and the Spirit against the flesh; and these things are contrary to one another, so that you do not do the things that you wish." (Galatians 5:17).

There is a battle within us whether between our flesh and our spirit. They are diametrically opposed to one another. The spirit wills one thing and the flesh another. The flesh has robbed countless millions of victory here on earth and of reward in heaven. The flesh is connected to the fallen world, which lies under Satan's control. It can be our closest enemy.

Let us be honest. Do you find it easy to pray all the time? How about to fast? Do you wake up every morning thinking, "I would love to fast today?" Unlikely if you are flesh and blood like the rest of us! I have learned that in my weakness God makes me strong. In other words, when I know it is right to pray or to fast and yet my flesh does not want to, I simply explain the situation to God. "Lord!" I say, "You need to help me. I need to pray, I want to pray, my friends and family need me to pray, the lost world will remain lost unless I pray, BUT I just don't feel like it! You need to do something in me God. You need to strengthen me. I can't do this alone… etc". Once after spending five minutes telling the Lord that I did not want to pray I realised that I was in fact praying - prayer is after all communing with God! As we all know once you are through the flesh barrier, you are able to press on into serious intercession.

When motor cars were first invented they were not equipped with keys and ignitions. Rather the driver had to reach under the bonnet and with a large spanner-like bar start the engine manually. If the engine was cold, this could mean a lot of energy and sweat was needed to get it going. Getting into the spirit of prayer can be like this. You have to start out with grit-like determination but once the engine runs you can motor for hours! When you enter into the spirit of intercession you are carried along by the energy of heaven, divine petroleum, to pray through until victory comes.

Jesus has many lovers of His heavenly kingdom, but few bearers of His Cross. He has many seekers of comfort, but few of tribulation. He finds many companions of His table, but few of His fasting. All desire to rejoice with Him, few are willing to undergo anything for His sake. Many follow Jesus that they may eat of His loaves, but few that they may drink of the cup of His passion. Many are astonished at His miracles, few follow after the shame of His Cross. Many love Jesus so long as no adversities happen to them. Many praise Him and bless Him, so long as they receive comforts from Him. But if Jesus hides Himself and withdraws a little while, they fall either into complaining or into too great dejection of mind.

Thomas á Kempis
German monk
1380–1471

3rd PRICE Principle
The prize is worth the price.

What is the prize for a life dedicated to winning others for Christ?

Firstly nothing can be more rewarding than spending eternity with those whom we have won for Christ. Knowing that we have been instrumental in the salvation of others is prize enough.

Secondly living a life full of purpose here on earth is again a great recompense. So many people drift through life wondering what it is all about. It is a great privilege and joy to know what matters in heaven's eyes and to dedicate ourselves to that end.

However, the Bible also reveals a third and much greater reward.

"Finally there is laid up for me a crown of righteousness which the Lord, the righteous judge, will give to me on that Day and not only to me but to all who have loved his appearing" (2 Tim 4:8)

"Blessed is the man who endures temptation for when he has been approved he will receive the crown of life which the Lord has promised to those who love him." (Jam 1:12)

The prize that Christ has on offer to his people is a glorious heavenly crown. A crown represents authority and power. The one who wears the crown sits upon a throne. The one who sits on the throne wields the power and has authority. A crown is much more than a pretty hat! True it is beautiful to look at and expensive in the making but what really makes a crown special is the significance that it holds.

In my home nation of the United Kingdom, our head of State is the Queen of England. However, her position has now become symbolic as the real power rests with the Prime Minister and with Parliament. Not so in heaven. Jesus is the King of kings and therefore the ultimate authority and power. Yet for Him to be King of kings there must also be kings in heaven. There are others who, due to their heavenly responsibilities, wield various levels of power and authority.

The Queen of England received her crown through her hereditary line. Not so with the crowns of heaven. There are no such preferred families. The prizes are given to those who have paid the price. The crowns are given to those who win the race.

Jesus taught, in the parable of the talents, that the faithful servants would receive cities to rule over in His Kingdom. It is clear that those who have been faithful with their talents are rewarded in His coming Millennial Kingdom. These people will be in His government. They are those whom He can entrust with the governing of His Kingdom. This is no small matter. What could be a greater honour than sitting with Christ and reigning with Him?

This honour does not go to all believers. Salvation is a gift of grace but the reward is given according to our works.

"And, behold, I come quickly; and my reward is with me, to give every man according as his work" (Rev 22:12)

What we do on earth is the measure stick for our reward in heaven.

When I studied at university I knew that by gaining a decent degree I would be in a good position to find a good job and gain a good salary. Hence in my third year I buckled down to some serious study. The prize of a degree was worth the price I needed to pay. Like students at university if we want the highest rewards we must put in the best work. The top prizes only go to those who pay the price of self-discipline and hard work.

Would you go to work if you were never paid? People do not spend hours of each day labouring in an office or work site simply to feel good. They have a goal in mind. They are exchanging the hours of life that God gave them for a salary that will enable them to provide for their families and do things they dream of doing.

Likewise God offers rewards for our working for Him. It is not that He has to reward us. (Simply to be saved is more than enough for me!) But, out of His goodness He desires to reward those who are faithful to do His will. He made mankind in such a way that we respond to the opportunities to win prizes and be promoted. Athletes train night and day to win positions on podiums. Businessmen put in extra hours to perfect their work in the hope of promotion.

When people see the rewards He has for those who are faithful they completely readdress the way they spend their lives. The way you live your life today determines your rewards tomorrow.

The centre of God's will for our lives is to fill the earth with sons in His image and likeness. Be faithful to do that and He is faithful to reward (Heb 11:6). He has laid up a crown for each one of us. Sadly due to negligence many people never fulfil the purpose of God for their lives. Others start strong but finish weak. Hence Jesus' warned:

"I am coming quickly, Hold fast to what you have that no one may take your crown." (Rev 3:11)

The apostle Paul taught that all of our works would be tested by fire at the judgment seat of Christ (1Cor 3:12-15). He likens our works to gold, silver and precious stones or wood, straw and hay. The first materials are purified by fire but the latter set materials are burned by fire. Only works that are done with the right heart and in accordance to his plan will be rewarded. It is these precious materials that will be moulded and made into the crowns that believers wear in His Kingdom. Your works here determine your position there. Do not think that death will change you into an all-spiritual committed and zealous minister of God. If you die immature, you will arrive in heaven immature. The Lord is not likely to entrust the powers of His Kingdom into immature hands!

Finally it is interesting to note that Paul mentioned that his own spiritual sons were his joy and his crown (Phil 4:1). Believers are referred to as living stones and the precious possession of God (1Pet 2:5, 9). Crowns are made from precious materials, stones, and gems. In other words, the crown you receive directly represents the quantity and quality of your spiritual children, according to the opportunities that God has given to you in life.

Friend, start now before it's too late. Dedicate your life to winning the lost and training them to be mighty men and women of God. You will thank me for such advice when you arrive in heaven and see the reward God has for you!

"We shall have all eternity in which to celebrate our victories, but we have only one swift hour before the sunset in which to win them."
Robert Moffat

PRAYER Principles

"It seems God can do nothing except through prayer."
John Wesley

There is a story of a captain of a ship that floundered in the high seas. As the ship began to sink the captain summoned all the passengers up onto the main deck, and he said to them, "Friends, there is nothing we can do to save the ship!" Then he asked, "Does anybody here know how to pray for a miracle?" Silence swept through the crowd until a young man at the back lifted up his hand and called out, "Captain, I do!" And the captain replied, "Good! We are one lifejacket short!"

1st PRAYER Principle:
HUMAN INTERCESSION LEADS TO DIVINE INTERVENTION.

It's a comical story but one with a serious point hidden in the humour – prayer can work miracles. Prayer helps you do what you can't do. Prayer invites God to get involved in your life. Prayer is really an invitation for divine power to come into human circumstance. Prayer can mean the difference between life and death. Prayer can mean the difference between success and failure. Prayer unleashes heaven's power to help you fulfil heaven's purpose.

"The earnest (heartfelt, continued) prayer of a righteous man makes tremendous power available [dynamic in its working]." (James 5:16b AMP)

Do your evangelistic efforts sometimes end in frustration? Have your words failed to penetrate peoples' hearts? Like throwing peas against a brick wall, do your words bounce back! Obviously if people do not want to listen, we cannot force them. But if the fields are ripe, then why are we not able to easily bring in the harvest?

> *"If you are strangers to prayer you are strangers to power."*
> Billy Sunday - Evangelist

Prayer gets divine power involved to bind demonic influences. Prayer prepares the soil of the heart to receive the seed of the word of God. Prayer sets the Holy Spirit in action. If you don't pray the Holy Spirit cannot act on your behalf. The Holy Spirit is directed by God in answer to prayers made in Jesus' name.

> *If believers don't pray,*
> *the Holy Spirit cannot act!*

A lack of prayer reveals a dependency in your own ability. Yet bringing people to Christ is the work of the Holy Spirit not the work of our own human strength. Through our own ability we can become good communicators, we can be witty and amusing, but unless the Holy Spirit is involved you will not be able to convict a person of sin and convince them of their need of Christ. This is divine work in us.

"And when He has come, He will convict the world of sin, of righteousness, and of judgment" (Jn 16:8)

"That which is born of the flesh is flesh, and that which is born of the Spirit is spirit." (Jn 3:6)

Prayer attracts the power of God. "Earnest prayer makes tremendous power available" (Jm 5:16b). It is as if prayer produces a cloud of anointing in you. Now, when you speak, God's power is released with your words. In this way the Lord confirms your words through the signs and wonders that accompany them (Mk 16:20).

2ND **PRAYER** PRINCIPLE:
PRAY AND YOU'LL BE LED, DON'T PRAY AND YOU'LL BE DRIVEN.

"Brother, if you would enter that Province, you must go forward on your knees."
Hudson Taylor – missionary to China.

In the mid 1990's I spent three years working in the Philippines, initially as a businessman and latterly as a full time missionary on some of the most remote islands in the world. The capital Manila is a hugely polluted metropolis of 10 million people, many of whom live in shanty towns. I hardly knew where to start my ministry or how to go about it. I distinctly remember falling on my knees and praying, "Lord I don't know anyone in this great city, but you know everybody." And "Lord, I don't know anything about them, but you know everything about them! So lead me to the people who You want to minister to." Then I stood up and strode off down town.

"The steps of a good man are ordered by the Lord" (Ps 37:23)

I had never experienced such heat and humidity combined and such a mass of people thronging the streets. Thousands of foreign faces flowing past me and somewhere in amongst them there was, I believed, a person that God specifically wanted me to talk to. How was I to recognise him? What was I to say anyhow?

"Hello!"
I stopped and looked up at a young man right in front of me as people streamed past either side. He was smiling from ear to ear.
"Hi!" I replied rather tentatively.
"Are you looking for anywhere in particular?" he asked.
"Well as a matter of fact I'm looking for you!"
"You're looking for me?" he replied in amazement
"Yes"; I said with more confidence.
"But you don't know me!"
"I don't know you, but I have a friend who does!"
"You have a friend who knows me?" he asked incredulously.

"Yes and He told me to give you this message." I continued.
I reached down into the hip bag that I was carrying and pulled out a Bible. When he saw it he exclaimed: "Oh no! You're one of those Christians." He went on, "I don't what to hear about religion. I came to talk to you because you're a Westerner, and I love to drink with foreigners. I'm a big drinker;" he said with a smirk.
To his surprise I said, "I love to drink too!"
"You do?" He exclaimed. "You're a strange kind of Christian!" And with that he led me off to a local bar that he frequented.
When we had sat down the young man, whose name I discovered was Obet, asked me what I would like to drink.
"I'll have some living water please," I replied.
"What? I've never heard of that!" The barman hadn't either.
"Don't worry. Then I'll have some heavenly wine," I offered.
Obet asked, "What? What is this heavenly wine? What is this living water?"
"The answer to that is the message of my friend," I explained. "God wants you to know that you should not waste away your life drinking alcohol but to be full of life by drinking His living water. What He has will satisfy you to such an extent that you will never look for contentment elsewhere!"

Obet was the first man that I baptised in Manila and he proved to be a key friend and prolific evangelist. Sometime afterwards whilst I was preparing to leave the capital to go and work in the smaller islands further south, Obet popped in to see me. He said, "Giles, I want to be baptised in the Holy Spirit right now!" I had an appointment scheduled and needed to leave. I said, "My friend I don't have time now." But Obet persisted. "Quickly!" I said, "Step inside. Stick your hands in the air!" Then I prayed, "Father, fill my brother with the Holy Spirit and with fire!" Immediately he burst out speaking in heavenly tongues! There he was standing in my open doorway, pouring his heart out to God in the most marvellous language! But I was now late for my appointment. I pushed him into the elevator and he headed off into the street shouting praises to God to surprised passers-by as he went!

Remember the point of this story - pray and you'll be lead: don't pray and you'll be driven.

> *If we are not praying then really we are playing.*
> *If we are not praying, then we are probably straying.*

Too many Christians are driven by circumstances and situations rather than led by the Lord. People charge about just below the stress line, struggling to make sense out of life, ever-hoping that someday they will achieve their goals for life. My advice is to pray first - pray before you stray and pray before you say! It is a case of pray now or pay later! God has divine connections lined up for you. He has people waiting in each place to receive you. Pray and He will lead you to them. If you make Him your living Shepherd He will led you to green pastures!

> *You can either be strong before God and weak before men*
> *or weak before God and strong before men.*

The man who does not pray demonstrates his reliance on himself, his trust in himself and his pride in his own ability. The man who prays demonstrates his dependency of God and his revelation of the source of God's power. The first man is weak before men and strong before God. The second is weak before God but mighty when he stands up before men.

That's perfect partnership. We know we cannot build His Kingdom in our power, so we pray for His power. Then we rise up to "be strong in the Lord, and in the power of his might" (Eph 6:10), and in the knowledge that we are God's chosen vessels to destroy the works of the enemy (1Jn 3:8). We are the mighty army of the Lord. We are God's men of faith and power for this hour. We have the greater power within us (1Jn 4:4) and the gates of Hades shall not prevail against us (Mt 16:18).

> *"I get on my knees and I pray like it all depends on God, and then I get on my feet and I run like it all depends on me."*
> Charles Finney – 19th Century American revivalist

Moses encountered God and became a deliverer. Joshua lingered in the presence of God and became a conqueror. Jacob wrestled with God and became Israel the prince and father of the 12 tribes. David poured out his heart to God in psalms and prayers and became a mighty king and leader. The promises of God and position in His Kingdom have always been the result of a lifestyle of prayer.

*Preaching without prayer
is like having a detonator without explosives.
Whereas preaching without prayer
is like having a explosives without a detonator!*

Some people pray and do not preach. Others preach and do not pray. A recent national survey in the USA discovered that many pastors pray less than 10 minutes a week. The devil has a strategy to disassociate these two fundamental disciplines. Preaching without prayer is like having a detonator without explosives! Whilst praying without preaching is like having explosives and no detonator.

Every member of the Body of Christ should be doing both. Specialists departments such as intercessory teams, preaching teams, might seem like a good idea, but they have actually robbed the church of potency and power. We are all called to be a holy priesthood (1Pt 2:9) and the duty of each priest is to communicate with God and communicate with man.

*We should talk to God about men
before we talk to men about God*

When my wife Silvia was single she prayed in much detail for a certain type of husband. One of her requests was for her future husband to be at least five years older than her. Having prayed, she sensed the Holy Spirit say to her that her husband's birthday would be a sign for her.

Some years later she and I met at a Fire Conference hosted by the champion German evangelist, Reinhard Bonnke. During our first conversation the subject came around to her birthday. When she told me her birthday was

12th September, I exclaimed; "That's amazing so is mine!" For Silvie this was a sign from God. For me it was a blessing from God as from henceforth I have never had to worry about forgetting my wife's birthday! The point is if you pray, coincidences like that happen, but if you don't pray, they don't! I had gone to the Fire Conference seeking more fire, but God gave me a fire-carrier in the form of my wife. If you ask God for silver He will give you gold!

God has organised God-appointments for each one of us all over town. When the apostle Paul was being given a hard time on his arrival in Corinth, God spoke to him in a night vision and confirmed to him that He had many people in that city waiting to hear from Paul (1 Co 18:8). It is the same for you. If you pray, you won't stray. If you pray, God will pave the way. He will lead you to those who need you. He is the Lord of the harvest and knows exactly where to begin to reap.

3RD PRAYER PRINCIPLE:
DIVINE INTIMACY DETERMINES PUBLIC MINISTRY.

If you talk to God face to face, His glory will stay upon you. Moses spoke with God face to face on Mount Sinai and when he came down from the mountain the glory of the Lord shone so brightly upon him that the Israelites could not look at him. Instead he needed to wear a veil over his face whenever he spoke to them. It could well be said that Moses could easily light up a room and change the atmosphere of a place. Why? Because the anointing of God was upon him.

If there is little anointing on a minister's life it is a sign that there is little prayer in his life. Someone once sai̇   ˙˙˙ never be bigger than your prayer life. The apostle Paul recom

Children are the fruit of the intimacy between man and woman. ˙˙˙˙˙ spiritual children are the fruit of intimacy between God and man. Jesus taught that if a branch abides in the vine it will naturally bear fruit (Jn 15). The only reason for not bearing fruit is being separate from the vine. In other words if a believer stays connect to his source through prayer, he will naturally bear fruit. The life-force of Christ flowing through him it is only natural that his fruit will be other Christians made in the same image and likeness.

One day on my way home I stopped off in a flower shop and bought my wife a large single red rose. The assistant carefully wrapped it for me and I headed home happily. Just before I gave it to my wife, I put the rose to my nose to savour its rich aroma but to my great disappointment it had no smell.

Not only was I disappointed, I also felt deceived. I had been sold a rose that promised an aroma but delivered none. I thought of returning to the shop to complain or get my money back. You see the image of a rose is one thing, but its smell is another. This image of the rose catches your eye and draws you towards it, but it is the smell of a rose as you place its petals near your nose that satisfies.

I believe that some of us believers are guilty of the same thing. We have the image of a Christian. After all we go to church on Sundays; we carry Bibles and speak in verses! But we lack the fragrance of Christ. Those who carry the fragrance immediately influence an environment. When they walk into a room, it is like a breath of fresh air comes with them. The effect is subtle but immediate. People lighten up and relax. Others get happy all of a sudden. Faith comes alive and people's expectations rise. Why? Because the fragrance or the presence of God is there.

You cannot see fragrance but you can see its effect. Likewise two Christians may look very similar but have very different effects on others. Very often we attract people. After all we have knowledge of the most profound words that the world has ever known. When we speak them people are often drawn to listen. But too often, if there is no substance to what we speak, if there is no anointing upon what we say, or if there is no sweetness in our words, those who were at first attracted now draw back. They may say; "You talk of joy and peace, but you have so little yourself!" They feel deceived. We have appeared as one thing but in reality are another. As

I rejected the rose, so too are Christians rejected for a lack of reality in substance in their lives.

Sure, there are always those that will prefer sin to righteousness and lies to truth. But there are others who are genuinely seeking for answers. The prayerless person is in danger of inoculating others against the truth. However, the prayerful person will not just attract them to Christ but will point them to the source of their fragrance upon their lives, Jesus, the sweet rose of Sharon. Spend time in prayer with him and not only will you be satisfied but you will find others will want to stay in your presence because of His fragrance on you.

"If you abide in Me, and My words abide in you, you will ask what you desire, and it shall be done for you." (Jn 15:7)

PRIORITY Principles

"You have nothing to do but save souls. Therefore spend, and be spent in this work. It is not our business to preach so many times a day, or to take care of this or that club or ministry, but to save as many souls as you can: to bring as many sinners as you possibly can to repentance, and with all your power to build them up in that holiness without which they can not see the Lord."

John Wesley

Imagine that a husband and wife decide to take their three children for a day out to have a picnic in the forest. They find a nice clearing, set up the picnic and spend a pleasant day together, taking in the sunshine whilst the kids play amongst the trees. When the sun begins to dip down, they pack up their things and call the kids to come. Two of their three children run back but the third fails to appear or to respond to their calls.

Do you think that those parents would have said to themselves; "Let's forget the third child! We have two out of three. Come, we are tired and it's getting dark, let's go home." Or would they have said, "Oh well, win one loose one!?" No! What would be the real response of theirs? They would search night and day to find that child! They would comb each inch of that forest. They wouldn't leave until they had found the lost child!

No doubt we would go to any measure to rescue a child from the terrors of being lost in a forest, therefore so much more should we engross ourselves in the hard work of rescuing millions from the horrors of being eternally lost in hell? We constantly need to be reminded of this uncomfortable reality for the devil works overtime to make us forget it.

"Oh, that I had a thousand lives, and a thousand bodies! All of them should be devoted to no other employment but to preach Christ to these degraded, despised, yet beloved mortals."

Robert Moffat

1st PRIORITY PRINCIPLE:
Make God's priority your priority.

So what is God's priority? Jesus said it best:

"For the Son of Man has come to seek and to save that which was lost." (Lk 19:10)

Whilst we may rejoice on the amount of people inside our churches, we must not forget the amount of people that are still on the outside of our churches. It is not so much an issue of how many are saved, but how many are still lost.

If the father in the above story, was thinking in business terms, he would have said to his wife; "Two out of three children – that's 66.6%. We have the market majority! Let's go home and celebrate". However, thankfully God does not think as a businessman but rather as a father. Hence for Him, if one child is lost, it is enough for him to leave the ninety-nine who are found, in order to find the lost one (Mt 18:12).

The Church is the only institution that exists for its non-members!

Sadly the issue of evangelism has slipped down the order of priorities in many churches. It has become a part-time extra activity for the few more zealous believers to engage in. It is certainly not the principle objective in each calendar year of the church. An astute observer once remarked that the Church is the only organisation that exists for its non-members. I can see his point.

Tragically many people miss the point in life as the following funny story reveals:

In the heart of the great city was a modern construction site surrounded by a large temporary fence. To enter or leave the site managers and labourers alike needed to pass through a security gate manned by a local guard. One evening a labourer came to check pushing a wheelbarrow in which was a carefully wrapped small white package. The guard, immediately suspicious, asked; "What is in the package?" The labourer responded; "It's just sawdust!" "I will need to check," said the guard, and he opened the small package only to find pure sawdust inside. At the same time the next day the same labourer checked out once again pushing a wheelbarrow in which was a carefully wrapped small white package. The guard, now doubly suspicious, asked to know its contents. "It's just sawdust!" said the labourer. Again the guard, refusing to believe, opened the package to see for sure. Indeed it was only sawdust. On the third day, the labourer once again checked out, pushing a wheelbarrow with a carefully wrapped small white package. The guard once again stopped him. He was bursting with curiosity. He knew the labourer was doing something wrong but he just could not think what it was. So he bargained with him saying; "Look, I promise not to report anything to the boss, but just tell me: What are you doing?" The labourer replied, "I am stealing wheelbarrows!"

What is the point of the story? The point is that many people miss the point! Many people never truly discover why on earth they are here. They don't know what their purpose is and therefore they do not know what to prioritise in life?

God's purpose for mankind was revealed when He made the first man and woman.

"And God blessed them and said to them 'Be fruitful and multiply. Fill the earth" (Gn1:28).

God is a father and commissioned man to generate a huge family of sons and daughters who bore God's image and likeness. The world was to be full of men and women in the image and likeness of God. God's purpose for man has never been changed, though it was frustrated through man's rebellion and fall. Through Christ, the second Adam, God is fulfilling His purpose as man and women from every nation on the earth are being born again into His family and raised up in His image and likeness. Hence Jesus commanded:

"Go therefore and make disciples of all nations" (Mt 28:19)

However, the enemy is subtle in his strategy in distracting us from our main calling in life. All too often man has been easily deceived into allocating the majority of his time, energy and resources to do things for God rather than generating children for God.

The first step in generating a family is giving birth. That is why evangelism, or spiritual birth, is the first priority. The second step is to raise our children to be healthy and mature, who then, in turn, will give birth to their own spiritual children.

> *The main thing*
> *is to make the main thing*
> *the main thing!*

What can be better for a man to arrive in heaven and find all his family and all his friends there? What could be worse than a man arriving in hell and finding his family and friends there? If this is the case we need to careful to focus our time and energy upon the things that really matter.

Success in God's terms is very different than the world terms. Successful believers are the ones who live with eternity in their minds. They know what the future holds and already are working to determine its outcome. In the light of eternity we can see clearly how our time should be spent. In light of heaven we can see clearly how our lives on earth should be prioritised.

> *Don't climb the wrong ladder in life only to find*
> *that it has been leaning against the wrong wall.*

2nd PRIORITY PRINCIPLE:
If you don't do the most important things first, you never get them done at all.

The reason most major goals are not achieved is that we spend our time doing second things first.

A university professor demonstrated this principle by placing a glass jar on a desk at the front of the classroom. He then filled the jar with large rocks and asked his students; "Is the jar full?"
"Yes sir" they replied.
"No, it is not!" said the professor. He then proceeded to pour into the jar a bucket of small stones and, having filled it, asked again; "Is the jar full?"
"Yes sir". Their response was the same.
"No, it is not!" said the professor. This time he filled the jar with sand, shook it so that the contents settled and then asked the same question.
"It must be full now!" said the students. But the professor picked up a jug of water and poured it into the glass jar until water was flowing over the edges.
Finally he asked again; "Is the jar full?"
"Yes, sir!" came the answer.
"You are correct" said the professor. Then he asked, "Now what does this demonstration teach us?
A keen student at the front of the class put up his hand and said; "Sir, as it was always possible to pack more materials into the jar, it is also possible to pack more activities than we think into our lives."
The rest of the students were suitably impressed by the response of their colleague and clapped heartily.
However, when the class had settled the professor said; "Actually this teaches us a much greater principle. The lesson is this – In order to get the big rocks into the jar I needed to put them in first, if I had tried to have put them in last there would not have been enough room. This teaches us that you must do the most important things in life first, for if you leave them for last you will never get them done!"

The bottom line is if we do not put evangelism high up on our annual agenda we will never find the time, energy or resources for it. Likewise if evangelism is not marked into your weekly agenda then you will always be too busy to find the time for it.

My personal cell group currently meets on a Thursday night each week. Our goal is to have many visitors come each week. Therefore we reserve every Wednesday evening to telephoning contacts or making visits to invite them to come the next day. Yet if we do not prioritise this time on Wednesdays we would never reap the fruit on Thursdays.

This simple yet profound principle can be applied to other areas of life. For example with prayer – if you do not pray as a priority each day, you will find you have no time for it. Secondly in tithing or in saving money – if you do not organise these transactions when you first receive your pay check at the beginning of the month, you will probably not have enough money at the end of the month to do so. Likewise there are many fathers who have sincere intentions of spending more time with their families but, if this is not a priority, their plans are normally ship-wrecked by issues arising at work, and to the frustration of all the family they are consistently fail to spend time with those whom they love most.

In the early stages of my marriage I determined to reserve one evening every week to spend alone with my wife in order to develop our relationship. We might go out to dinner or watch a movie or go for an evening walk. But I have learned this – unless it is booked in my diary and made a priority, I never seem to have the time for it.

Friends, unless we prioritise speaking to friends about their need of a saviour, we will never find the time or the energy to do this. We will neglect the most important reason for being here on planet earth.

Here are 3 steps to help you plan out your priorities:

1. Set goals

Setting goals helps people to focus on their priorities. In choosing your goals you need to find the balance between putting too much pressure and too little pressure on yourself, your cell group or church at large. Pressure can be a good thing in that it helps people to operate at a higher level. But too much pressure, through unrealistic goals, can be a real de-motivator. That said, I believe that we must always be trying to achieve goals that are beyond our natural capacity - by doing so we will always de dependant on God. Faith starts where ability stops. God is a rewarder of those who have faith in His miracle-working power. If your goals make people sit down and relax, then they are too small. If your goals first must people walk away briskly, then they are too big. But if your goals first inspire and then bring people to their knees, then you have pitched it just right. How many people do you want to win this year? How many members do you want to have as a part of your church this year?

Once you have established your goals, break them down into bite-size parts. To answer this you must consider questions such as: How many people do you need to win per month? What percentage responds to your invitations to a church evangelistic event? What percentage converts as a result? What percentage joins your church as a result? If you have an average of 7 people per cell group, how many new cell groups do you need to start? Therefore how many new cell leaders will you need to train? Etc.

2. Set dates

Have you ever noticed that when you a booked to go on holiday, how much it is possible to achieve before the departure date arrives. Why? Because you know that you will not be able to do anything after the date arrives so you focus on your priorities and limit wasted time.

Without setting dates, most people procrastinate. When the pressure comes on them they simply put off what needs to be done for a later date. But when the date is fixed, the pressure helps them to resolve issues.

Set your growth plans to a fixed date. For instance plan that your cell group reaches ten people by the end of the 2nd quarter (June). Plan to have a leader in training operating by the end of the 3rd quarter (September). And plan a cell group harvest party at the end of the year in which the group multiplies into a two with a minimum of 6 people in each group.

3. SET ACCOUNTABILITY

Goals are great and dates even better, but without some form of accountability, these can be changed too easily. To really achieve your vision, it is best to hold yourself accountable to someone else either within your organisation or without. By reporting in regularly to state how well you are doing in accordance to your goals, it is easier to keep focussed and stay on track. By doing so you can address hindrances early on rather than letting them compound with time and therefore be harder to overcome. This can also prove to be a great source of motivation for you and your team. When you report back that you have reached your goals, it is a great time to celebrate!

What gets measured gets done!

3RD PRIORITY PRINCIPLE:
YOU WILL EITHER LIVE BY PRIORITIES OR BY PRESSURES!

The downside of not prioritising is a life full of pressure. People who are constantly in a rush are normally people who have not learned to prioritise. They are people who live according to circumstances that arise rather than God-given vision. They are reactive rather than proactive.

> *Things that matter the most must never be*
> *at the mercy of things that matter least*

If we make it a regular priority to fast and pray for our families and friends, we will have many more opportunities to witness to them over the course of their lives. Sadly many people wait until tragedy strikes or old age and impending death approaches before they get into prayer action.

I have made it a rule to set time aside every year to pray and to fast for my family and friends to be saved. Some people think that if they have prayed once then that is enough. I believe that we should pray until the answer comes. Jesus said, "Ask and it shall be given; seek and you shall find; knock and the door will be opened" (Mt 7:7). In the original Greek these verbs are written in the present continuous. In other words the literal translation is "ask and keep asking; seek and keep seeking" and "knock and keep knocking".

Take control of your life! Discipline your body! Don't serve your body; rather make your body serve you. The flesh hates to pray and make the effort to evangelise. It would much rather keep you at home watching TV and eating chocolate biscuits. Your lost family and friends depend upon you, even though they may not know it. Rise up and get into action. Make evangelism your highest priority. You will be thankful in heaven that you made the effort on earth.

The horrific film Schindler's List portrays the life of a German businessman who had saved more than 1000 Jews from the concentration camp and certain death by employing them in his factory. There is a scene at the end of the film in which Schindler himself breaks down in tears when he realises that if he had given more and done more he could have saved even more people from such a terrible death. I wonder if Christ will have to wipe away tears of regret from our eyes when we enter into eternity and realise we could have done more and therefore saved more.

Let us make our minds up today, that evangelism is our priority and we must stick to it through thick and thin. To be committed is to continue to do something whether you feel like it or not. You do it out of principle. You do it because you know it is right and it has to be done.

PERSPECTIVE Principles

"Study the history of revival. God has always sent revival in the darkest days. Oh, for a mighty, sweeping revival today!"
Adrian Rogers

1st PERSPECTIVE Principle:
IF YOU CAN SEE THE BIGGER PICTURE YOU WILL ACT IN A BIGGER WAY!

For many of us, it seems as if it is almost impossible for certain family members, friends or acquaintances to be saved. Some seemed to be so steeped in religion and tradition, others in worldliness, that there is no way for the light of the Gospel to penetrate. But I believe that we hold a powerful key in our hands that could unlock even the hardest heart. We will discover this in this chapter on perspective.

To have a different perspective is to look at the same thing from a different point of view. To have greater perspective is to be able to see the bigger picture, or the greater scheme of things. Our perspective determines the way we behave towards people and situations.

Firstly allow me to illustrate the importance of perspective through the following humorous letter. It was written by a girl, in her first year of college, who was desperately trying to gain the sympathy of her parents:

Dear Mum and Dad,

Since I left for college I have been remiss in writing and I am sorry for my thoughtlessness in not having written before.
I will bring you up to date now but before you read on, please sit down. Are you sitting down? Don't read on unless you are....
I am getting along pretty well now. The skull fracture and concussion that I got when I jumped out of my dormitory window when it caught on fire shortly after my arrival here has pretty well healed. I only get those sick headaches once a day.

Fortunately the fire in my dormitory and the jump was witnessed by an attendant at the petrol station. He ran over, took me to hospital and continued to visit me there. When I got out of the hospital I had nowhere to live because of the burnt-out conditions of my room, so he was kind enough to invite me to share his basement bedroom flat with him. It's sort of small, but cute.

He is a very fine boy and we have fallen deeply in love and are planning to get married. We haven't set an exact date yet but it will be before my pregnancy begins to show. Yes, Mum and Dad, I'm pregnant! I know how much you are looking forward to being grand-parents and I know you will welcome the baby and give it the same tender care and devotion that you gave me when I was a child.

The reason for the delay in our marriage is that my boyfriend has a minor infection which I carelessly caught from him. I know, however, that you will welcome him into our family with open arms. He is kind and, although not well educated, he is ambitious. Although he is of a different race and religion than ours, I know that your often expressed tolerance will not permit you to be bothered by that.

In conclusion, now that I have brought you up to date, I want to tell you that there was no dormitory fire. I did not have concussion or skull fracture. I was not in the hospital, I am not pregnant, I am not infected and there is no boyfriend in my life.

However, I am failing history and science and I wanted you to see these marks in their proper perspective!

Through her letter this girl forced her parents to see things from a different perspective, or in other words, to see the bigger picture. Similarly the Lord often challenges us to see things differently in order for us to have the faith we need to conquer.

We all know people who are sinful and selfish. But try not to get bogged down in these issues. Be gracious. See beyond this. Behind the self-centeredness that spoils a person, is a heart crying out for love and acceptance. I am not suggesting you gloss over the fact that people are sinners, but rather that you try to see people through the blood of Jesus.

After the apostle Paul had encountered the risen Christ on the road to Damascus he was led by hand, due to being struck blind, to the house of Judas on Straight Street. An angel appeared to a believer by the name of Ananias who lived the same city and instructed him to visit Paul. When he arrived he laid hands on him and said:

"Brother Saul, the Lord Jesus, who appeared to you on the road as you came, has sent me that you may receive your sight and be filled with the Holy Spirit." (Acts 9:17)

Ananias did not criticise him for his sins and chastise him for his stoning of Stephen. Likewise he did not refuse to meet up with such a notorious persecutor of the church. Rather he went directly to him and addressed him "Brother Paul!" He saw him through the blood of Jesus as a blood-bought-sinner-saved-by-grace-called-to-be-a-saint!

We need to have the proper perspective with our unbelieving friends. It is true they are lost and without hope (Eph 2.12). It is true that they are dead in trespasses and sins (Eph 2:1). But it is also true that Jesus is a friend of sinners (Lk 7.34).

2ND PERSPECTIVE PRINCIPLE:
A PROPER PERSPECTIVE IS TO SEE AS GOD SEES.

Too much pessimism has led too many men into making serious mistakes. And perhaps part of our pessimism comes because we are too close to ourselves to see in proper perspective.
Richard L. Evans

When Joshua took over from Moses as the leader of the Israelite people, he was immediately confronted with a big challenge. In order to enter into the Promised Land, his weary wandering people needed to first overcome the inhabitants of the city of Jericho, which, with its huge fortified walls, loomed above them majestically on the horizon. To a people who had spent forty years living in tents in the desert, and who were ill-equipped for battle, it would have appeared near impossible to conquer. Looking up at those big stone walls, hearing the taunts of the enemy soldiers above, and realising the difficulty his own men would have to scale the walls or smash through the city gates, Joshua would have been tempted to turn back.

But God spoke to Joshua as he contemplated his strategy and said some seemingly ridiculous words to him;

And the Lord said to Joshua: "See! I have given Jericho into your hand, its king, and the mighty men of valour. (Joshua 6:2)

With his physical eyes Joshua would have only seen obstacles and opposition, but God was calling him to look deeper, through the eyes of faith, which sees as God sees. To God, mountains are molehills! In comparison to God's majesty and strength, these huge walls and powerful army were like pieces of Lego and plastic soldiers.
"With men it is impossible, but not with God; for with God all things are possible." (Mk 10:27)

> *"Faith is to believe what we do not see; and the reward of this faith is to see what we believe."*
>
> St Augustine

Once Joshua could see the situation as God saw the situation, he received the faith to follow what the Lord instructed him to do. Led by the priests carrying the Ark of the Covenant, the Israelites marched around the city once for six days, and then seven times on the seventh day in absolute silence. They then let out a mighty shout and, as they blew their battle bugles, the walls of the city came tumbling down. Such faith and obedience has always released heaven's angelic force to accomplish God's will. This kind of faith is birthed through having the right perspective.

Without the right perspective you cannot have faith. Faith is to see with your spiritual eyes the promises of God before you can see them with your natural eyes. When you look through eyes of faith, you are able to appropriate the promises of God.

When you consider the unsaved members of your family and friends, does it seem like it is nearly impossible for them to surrender to Christ? Are they closed to spiritual things, independent, irreligious, etc? In the natural they may seem the most unlikely people to convert to Christ. We are often tempted to think that those steeped in sinful lifestyles would never respond to the Gospel. However, God is able to penetrate the hardest heart and to enlighten the darkest mind. If He saved you, He can save anyone! The greatest sinners can become the greatest saints!

> *"Faith sees the invisible, believes the unbelievable, and receives the impossible."*
> Corrie ten Boom

The Apostle Paul, formerly known as Saul of Tarsus, described himself as "the chief of sinners" (1 Tm 1:15). This man dedicated himself with youthful zeal in denouncing the teachings of the early Christians and imprisoning their leaders, even giving his approval to the stoning of Stephen (who consequently became the first Christian martyr). Yet through the fervent prayers of the church (Acts 4:23-31), the Lord Jesus appeared to Saul on the road to Damascus, and his life was totally transformed.

With God all things are possible. Some years ago the Lord led me to hold a series of evangelistic events in Leicester Square, the centre of London's night-life district. Thousands of people come to the theatres, clubs and bars here every night of the week. Drunkenness and drugs are rife. I hired one of the theatres and held an event called the "Midnight Hour". Starting at 10pm we invited Christian bands and drama groups to perform, and at midnight I stood up to give a clear Gospel talk and an appeal on the hour of midnight. At the time many well-meaning brothers questioned my wisdom for going into such a worldly environment and holding such late night meetings. Yet the Lord burned a scripture on my heart which gave me great faith to press forward:

"But where sin abounded, grace abounded much more," (Rm 5:20b)

No matter how much sin people are in, the blood of Jesus has paid the price for them all. No matter what a person's vices and addictions, the power of the Holy Spirit is able to break their enslaving chains. No sin is too grave, no devil is too great - Christ has broken the back of the devil's power.

The Lord's dominance was wonderfully displayed when Jesus encountered the demoniac in Garasenes (Mk 5:1-13). This man was possessed by a legion of demons. A Roman legion was comprised of 6000 men. The likelihood of victory can seem remote at odds of 6000:1. But one command from Jesus and the demons fled, each of them filling a massive heard of pigs and driving them into the sea.

What is your perspective? I am not just saying you simply need to have a positive perspective. (Positive thinking only goes so far.) I am saying you need to have a heavenly perspective. You need to see the bigger picture. You need to see as God sees. You need to think as God thinks. The person who acts on the promises of God sees the glory of God. We must remember that God "is able to do exceedingly abundantly above all that we ask or think, according to the power that works in us," (Ep 3:20)

The early church prayed for those who were opposed to the Gospel (At 4:23-31, Mt 5:44). Their results were extraordinary; many converted, including thousands who had called for Jesus to be crucified on that fateful day in front of Pontius Pilate.

My friends, we cannot be led by sight; we must be led by faith. We cannot be led by natural thinking and our limited human perspective. We must be led by spiritual thinking and an unlimited divine perspective.

"We have a God who delights in impossibilities."
Billy Sunday

Your friends CAN be saved! Your family CAN be saved! Stop wondering if they will make it and start believing that they will be!

When I preach to crowds, before I pray with those who want to accept Christ, I say "I believe there are many people here who will receive Christ as the Lord and Savour. There are young people and old people, local people and foreigners, men and women, boys and girls, people to my left and people to my right, people at the front and people at the back, who all are going to come down here to the front and join God's heavenly family!"

We must believe that God is going to use to use us to win the people to Christ every time we preach. Every time we open our mouths in His name we must believe that His power will manifest to save, heal and set free. This must be our perspective. We must learn that if we believe then we receive! Be careful not to be double-minded or you will receive nothing from the Lord (Jm 1:7). Don't stop believing, don't stop praying, and don't stop preaching! If it takes a lifetime of prayer and preaching to get people saved, it would still be worthwhile.

3RD PERSPECTIVE PRINCIPLE:
YOUR OBSTACLES ARE YOUR OPPORTUNITIES.

When David stood before Goliath, what sort of perspective did he have? The giant was almost 11ft 4" (3.5m) tall. His spear was the size of a weaver's beam and his coat of bronze armour weighed 125 pounds (56kg). But David did not compare the giant with himself but with God. He knew that the battle was not his but it was the Lord's (1 Sm 17:47). Negative perspective says: "He is so big; I can't win with only a sling shot". Positive perspective says: "He's so big; I can't miss with my sling shot!"

There is a well-known story about two shoe-salesmen based in Europe who visited Africa many years ago to study the shoe market there. After their visits one salesman reported to his boss "Boss! In Africa nobody wears shoes! We will never sell any there!" The other salesman reports the same state of affairs but his prognosis is very different. He says, "Boss! In Africa nobody wears shoes! We will sell millions of pairs there". I don't know if the story is true but it certainly reveals two contrasting perspectives which in turn lead to two very different responses to the situation.

My point is that if you think nobody will be converted through your ministry then you are probably right nobody will! But if you believe that you have the words of eternal life and that hundreds if not thousands are going to listen to you and be saved, then you are probably right too! The choice is yours.

> *A negative perspective makes mountains out of molehills.*
> *A positive perspective makes molehills out of mountains.*

Do you believe that God can move in your family, your city, your nation? Do not underestimate the power of God. When the hand of God came upon Ezekiel, he was taken to a valley of dry bones, where the Lord asked him if the dry bones could live (Ez 37). Ezekiel's simple response was "Lord, you know". In other words, "Lord, You know they can! You know everything and everyone and have made all things. If you say they can live then they shall live!" Ezekiel's perspective was heavenly. In response to his faith, God instructed him to prophesy to the bones and the dry bones came together, clothed themselves in flesh and there grew a mighty army.

A person with a positive perspective prays and prophesies God's promises to come into being. We must play our part in the miracle process of bringing people who spiritually are like dry bones and clothing them in Christ so that they might become a mighty army for the Lord (Gal 3:27).

> *Man's impossibility is God's opportunity.*

When the hand of God came upon Ezekiel, he was led to Dry-bone Valley and not to Lush-grass Meadow! Most people want God to lead them to places where the churches are big, the community is prosperous and peaceful and life is easy. Yet the situation in Dry-bone Valley is very different. Here the churches are empty and the going is tough. Here only a miracle will do.

In scripture the "hand of God" refers to the Holy Spirit. In other words it was the Spirit of God that led Ezekiel to this difficult place. God had found in Ezekiel the type of faith that He could work with to transform a situation. Whilst the flesh will always lead you to a life of comfort and ease, the Spirit will often lead you into very difficult situations. Why? Because you have God's life transforming power within you, which is released, when you prophesy.

Maybe the city in which you live is a real "dead zone". Maybe you sense in your heart a call to go to a place where the people are hard and far away from God. Maybe you are the only believer in your family. Maybe you come from a long line of atheists or agnostics or hedonists. Maybe the only time your family goes to church is for weddings, funerals and the occasional Christmas midnight mass. Spiritually speaking it's a valley of dry bones. But man's impossibility is God's opportunity. He delights in making something out of nothing, in turning the impossible into the possible, in bringing life where there is only death. But he needs a person with the right perspective to work through.

The darkest hour is before the dawn

Ezekiel was not put off by the circumstances. He did not ask God to take him somewhere easier or to prophesy something a little less radical. Rather he remained full of faith. The man of faith really comes alive when faced with big problems. Whilst your circumstances can be terrible, you can be terrific. Never forget that you have a tremendous God who can transform any situation.

In your prayers you can say: "Lord, Your blood has paid the price for sins of my family, therefore I claim them for You in Jesus name!"

In your preaching you can say, "It does not matter where you have been and what you have done, because of where Jesus has been and what He has done. His grace is sufficient. He accepts you as you are!"

PREPARATION Principles

"Champions do not become champions when they win the event, but in the hours, weeks, months, and years they spend preparing for it. The victorious performance itself is merely the demonstration of the championship character."

Alan Armstrong

1st PREPARATION Principle:
WHEN OPPORTUNITY MEETS PREPARATION YOU FIND GOD'S FAVOUR.

The Bible teaches that our God has no favourites (Gal 2:6). His grace is freely and evenly distributed to everyone. Then how is it that some people seem to have tremendous favour on their lives? They seem to be in the right place, at the right time, when the opportunities come. They achieve so much. They seem to have a special touch upon their lives that makes the difference. I believe this is because they are prepared.

If you are not satisfied with the results you are achieving in life, don't look around for the problem, rather look within. Our external ministries are the result of our internal spirituality. Your outer world reflects your inner world. The bigger you are on the inside the more impact you will have on the outside. Jesus was a spiritual giant; therefore he could conquer the tests of this world.

There is the pain of self-discipline and the pain of regret

If you prepare yourself God can use you mightily. The problem for most people is not that opportunities do not come. Rather when opportunities do come, they either do not recognise them or are not ready to seize them.

The miracle through you is only ever as big as the miracle in you.

Most newly converted Christians are zealous for the Lord and zealous to convert others. With their eyes now opened they realise how much they have been saved from and how much they have been saved to. They want

If you fail to prepare, you are preparing to fail

God gives us special seasons of preparation. Jesus worked as a carpenter for all of his adult life until age 30 when he began to minister. During this time he was learning much more than simply how to make furniture! The Apostle Paul spent 7 years in Arabia in preparation. His missionary zeal burned brightly throughout his life because of the revelation he received during this precious time. God was putting fire in his bones!

We need to learn to recognise the seasons of life. Often God will draw you aside to work something into your character that you need for the future. Those people who do not embrace these seasons can end up burned out, cynical and depressed. There are those who go to work under-prepared and therefore get frustrated with their results. Others blame their circumstances and environment rather than taking an honest look at the lack of their own training and preparation.

Joseph was given an awesome dream that the sun, moon and stars would bow down to him. He sensed in his spirit that, despite being the second youngest son, his father and mother and brothers would all have to bow before him in the future. His dreams led him to believe that he would influence the whole world. When we convert to Christ we begin to dream too! We want to be used by God in a special way to touch and change the world.

But as Joseph discovered, it is one thing to receive the dream, it is another to fulfil the dream. To do that we need to be made of the sort of material that God can use. Joseph, the dreamer, needed to be moulded into Joseph, the hard-worker! God used his jealous brothers to sell him off as a slave to Egyptian merchants. Joseph's training course arrived with a thump!

God moulded and made this man through all his trials and tests. From being a favourite son he went to being a common slave and latterly to prison as an adulterer. Yet throughout this his character was formed. His faithfulness to a foreign employer was exemplary. His integrity was put to the test when to tell the whole world now!

Unfortunately there are always older Christians who tell them to calm down and by doing so throw water upon their fiery zeal. Rather we should fan their flames and, at the same time, train them in the ways of the Lord. All our converts are immediately encouraged to go on a Spiritual Maturity Course and then a Leadership Training Course. Having done these they then have the option of studying at the Bible Institute. In addition they will also be looked after by their cell leader and their "guardian angel" (person responsible to help them take their first steps) on a personal basis.

There are many reasons for such immediate and thorough training but one of them is undoubtedly because we want them to be effective evangelists. We realise that we must add wisdom to a young convert's zeal. Whilst zeal may open doors, it is wisdom that opens hearts.

> "He who wins souls is wise." (Pr 11:30b)

There are two sides to this proverb. Firstly it is wise to choose to be a soul-winner. Why? Because this is the very heart of the Father. The centre of His heart is that "none should perish, but all should come to repentance" (2 Pt 3:9). God's eternal desire is to fill the earth full of children made in His image and likeness (Gn 1:28). Hence Jesus' command was for us to "Go and make disciples of all nations" (Mt 28:18). Evangelism is the first step in the son-making process. Without the raw material we have nothing to mould into Christ's image.

Secondly you will need to employ wisdom if you want to be an effective soul winner. The fishermen who fish in the wrong place, with the wrong hook at the wrong time, will come home with nothing; even if his zeal keeps him working all day!

We realise that our young converts still have many relationships with unbelievers. We want to equip them as fast and as best as possible to win them over. Older Christians have less unbelieving friends and therefore have to work harder to evangelise.

Potiphar's wife tempted him in private. (How many men of God in the making have fallen at this test? Unlike Joseph, they shall never make their mark on history.)

Perhaps most godly of all, was his ability to forgive despite all the injustice that he suffered at the hands of his brothers, his employers, and his colleagues whom he helped in prison. He carried no grudges. He wished no-one evil. He was here to serve and believed that "all these things would turn out for good" (Rm 8:28). When his brothers discovered he was a prince in Egypt with the power to put them all to death, they feared for their lives. But Joseph had no such thoughts. He did not repay evil with evil but with blessing by not just sparing their lives but giving them land, food and safety. He saw the divine purpose behind their actions.

"I am Joseph your brother, whom you sold into Egypt. But now, do not therefore be grieved or angry with yourselves because you sold me here; for God sent me before you to preserve life. … And God sent me before you to preserve a posterity for you in the earth, and to save your lives by a great deliverance. So now it was not you who sent me here, but God; and He has made me a father to Pharaoh, and lord of all his house, and a ruler throughout all the land of Egypt." (Gn 45:5-8)

God purposefully kept Joseph out of the limelight until he was prepared for his prophetic task and rose to be effective prime minister in Egypt. But during his time in obscurity, what did Joseph do? Did he lick his wounds and feel sorry for himself? Did he complain that he was called for higher things than be a house slave or prison worker? No! Rather he diligently set about employing all of his gifts and abilities to the tasks at hand. Through it he became spiritually, physically and intellectually mature.

The secret for success in life is for a man to be ready when his time comes.

When the opportunity came there was only one man in the world who was able to seize it. Pharaoh needed a dream interpreted. His own counsel could not help him. But one of them knew of Joseph, a man who could be trusted, and who had the ability to interpret dreams. The rest is history.

His promotion was catastrophic. He went from prisoner to prime minister in a day!

When opportunity meets a person prepared, there you find the favour of God. Was his rise because God favoured him above others? Or was his rise because he had paid the price in developing his character and gifts to be used in God's timing?

2ND PREPARATION PRINCIPLE:
IT'S BETTER TO LOOK AHEAD AND PREPARE THAN TO LOOK BACK AND REGRET.

Noah built the ark when it was not raining! Many people wait for the rain to come and then react but it is too late - the opportunity has passed. There are many old people who are full of melancholy and regret in what should be the calm twilight of their lives. Regret comes as the result of missed opportunities and poor decisions. They know that they could have done more with their time. In contrast highly productive people are proactive people. They plan ahead in the knowledge that opportunities are bound to come. They want to be ready for that moment.

> "If you are proactive you focus on preparing, if you are reactive you focus on repairing."
>
> John Maxwell

If the Lord orders the steps of a good man, have you ever wondered where God is leading you? Think about it from a heavenly perspective. God above can see the sin, sicknesses and suffering of this world. His chosen way to resolve this problem is through the Body of Christ.

Be prepared! God is sending people your way. With every convert to Christianity, Christ has an extra heart to love through, extra hands to touch through, and an extra voice to speak through. Hence the Father directs our footsteps to those who are in need. He supernaturally leads us to meet people. The question is "Are you ready to meet these people?" Do you realise that God could have put the person you sit next to in the bus there?

Do you realise that you were offered that job, not simply because they needed your service or that you needed the money, but because God wanted you to win people there for Christ?

You are an ambassador of Christ, through whom God is pleading (2Cor 5:20). An ambassador is someone who is sent out into foreign territory to represent his homeland. You have been sent. We must cease from thinking simply on a natural plane and open our eyes to see the hand of God in all that you are doing and in every situation that you find yourself.

Many situations come our way in life that we did not choose. For instance you did not choose the colour of your eyes, your parents, your generation, your nationality, and your first language. But could it be that God chose it for you? You may even have been a mistake in the eyes of your parents, but you were no mistake for God. He had plans for you before the foundation of the earth. He knew what people would need in your land, in your generation and equipped you for active service. You are on divine assignment. Your mission field is all around you. Thousands of people are waiting for your words, your love, your wisdom. You are their hope. Without the message that you have, they will remain lost in darkness, searching for understanding, afflicted by demonic forces.

You don't have to wait for opportunities - if no doors are open then build a door!

Those who are really well prepared don't even need to wait for opportunities. If there are no doors open they simply build a door! Noah did not wait for his ship to come in, he built one! The Apostle Paul did not wait for churches to invite him to speak, he started new ones!

An evangelist friend rang me once and told me that he had been waiting for the right opportunity to witness to his neighbour. He waited and waited for the perfect time and opportunity. Sadly one day he received notice that his neighbour had suddenly died. Then he regretted waiting for right opportunities. The early church did not preach simply because they were invited to but rather because they were compelled to. They realised that God called them to be Proclaimers of Good News. Newscasters tell us the news every day on television, radio and the press. So too preachers should be "preaching in season and out of season" (2Tim 4:2) or, in other words, in times when people are ready to receive and times when they are seemingly disinterested.

There is the unforgettable story of Ian McCormack who was stung seven times by a highly venomous box jelly-fish. As the poison worked its way around his body, paralysing each part as it went, he realised he was about to die. There in his desperation he remembered a card that his mother had sent him years before as he set out on his prodigal travels. On the outside of the card was written "Jesus, the Light of the World". And on the inside she had penned in her on hand; "Son, remember it does not matter how far you go from the Lord, if you call out to Him, He will be there." His amazing story of dying and coming back to life having met with the risen Lord is inspirational for all of us who have put our hope in Christ.

Don't be a consumer Christian be a producer Christian

We need to be intentional evangelists. We need to go from being consumer Christians and become producer Christians. Consumers Christians are like clients. They come to church to get their weekly spiritual fix but little more. Producer Christians want to have fruit in their lives, they are dedicated to generating their own spiritual offspring and training their own disciples to be influential believers.

Many people remember to bring their Bibles to the service or the cell but they forget to bring people. We cannot do this unless we plan ahead, unless we are proactive. Few people are going to bang on your door and force there way in. I don't know of any fish that jump up into the fisherman's boat! We have to go and get them. We should all carry invitations with us if we are to be prepared for the divine encounters with people that God organises. It is amazing how far a smile and an invitation will go.

Planning ahead also involves developing a strong working knowledge of the Word of God. Too many Christians cannot explain the fundamentals of the faith. They know that they believe but they don't know why they believe, and they struggle to explain their faith in comprehensible terms. They are like those who live in a city and yet who cannot give directions to visitors. They have not taken time to learn the road names and to master the layout of the city.

Producer Christians have trained themselves to be Gospel specialists. During the Second World War a church minister was recruiting younger colleagues to join him working with the troops on the front lines. To choose his team he would ask the young minister to explain the Gospel to him in two minutes. If he could not do that in a clear and concise manner, he would not be chosen. Why? Because you never know how much time you have with a dying soldier.

3rd PREPARATION Principle:
GREAT COMMUNICATORS MAKE PROFOUND THINGS SIMPLE TO UNDERSTAND.

Imagine that you are headed out to have lunch with friends in a city you do not know. You've looked at the map, but the roads all seem different in reality. So after trying and trying you finally decide to stop and ask directions. Is it not incredible how many people give you such complicated instructions that you think to yourself "I will just drive in the direction he is pointing and ask someone else down there!" One local resident said to a lost driver "Well if I was going to where you are then I wouldn't start from here!"

So many people are terrible at giving directions. They may have lived for years in a city but still can't explain in simple terms how to get about. For a start many drivers, if they are anything like me, are reluctant to stop and ask for directions. We would prefer to drive for miles and miles trying to find the place on our own rather than stop and ask, despite being implored by our wives!

Much is the same in evangelism. Firstly many people are reluctant to stop and ask for directions. They may not have a clue about eternal and spiritual matters, but they would prefer to keep on driving on in life hoping they might find the place they are looking for. Few people come knocking on your door asking "How can I be saved?" or "What happens when I die?"

Therefore when people do finally stop and talk to us about such matters, we must be aware that, like the lost driver, these people are probably in a rush, tired and frustrated (otherwise they would not have stopped)! The last thing they need is a three page detailed description of the road ahead. They just need to know the key landmarks. Anything else and you will lose them!

We need to be able to present the Gospel in a simple and impacting manner so that lost, busy, frustrated people will be able to follow the directions and arrive at the destination.

Here are the four simple "signs" that I use to direct people along the Road of Salvation. (You can use this as a framework and add your own words instead of mine.)

THE ROAD TO SALVATION

1. RIGHTEOUSNESS

God is an awesome amazing being who existed before time even began. The Bible teaches us that He is holier than holy; that He is like a brilliant white light that has absolutely no darkness. In other words, He always thinks right, speaks right and acts right. God is also Life itself – everlasting, abundant, pure life. Everything He touches and makes bursts with life! When He made the heavens and the earth, He revealed what a creative powerful God He is.

God is also fatherly. This caused Him to create the original man and woman. He wanted to share His glory and blessings with a family of sons and daughter. For this reason he made mankind in His own noble image and likeness. He filled them full of His own life so they could live eternally and enjoy His presence forever. He also gave the man and the woman a desire to reproduce so that a huge family of God would be brought into existence.

That's why you and I are here.

(See Rev 22:11, Jer 23:6, 1John 1:5, Titus 1:2, Acts 10:34, Gen 1:28)

2. REBELLIOUSNESS

That was the plan but tragically for us things have gone terribly wrong. The Bible teaches that we have all sinned and fallen from God's standards. In other words, each of us has done things contrary to God's perfect commands. He told us to not lie and cheat, to not steal or kill, to not lust after others, and most of all to serve Him with all our hearts. But each us has preferred to try and live independently from God with little or no respect for His rules.

Because we have broken His laws we are criminals in the eyes of a just God. According to God's holy law crimes must be punished. The penalty of sin is death itself – physical, spiritual and eternal death.

We were created for life, but through our choice we are now destined for death. We are already dead spiritually (which is why our hearts are full of selfish desires), we will die physically in years to come, and worst of all, we will then die eternally, which is to be separated from God and all His goodness forever in a terrible place called hell!

(See Rom 3:19, 23, 6:23, Matt 7:17, Jer 17:9)

3. RANSOM

But just when all seems lost and it is clear that we are absolutely without any hope at all, the Bible shows us that God knew that we would sin and in His mercy and grace has made a way for us to escape this awful predicament.

It was never his desire that we should perish. Therefore God the Father sent God the Son to become Man, Jesus Christ, and on the cross at Calvary He took upon Himself our sins and the punishment of our sins. He died in our place!

It was as if we had a legal debt that we could not pay, but now Christ has paid it for us. That means we can walk away free. We no longer need to pay the punishment of our sins. God has acted both justly and also is Justifier of sinners. A new life is now on offer to us again.

(See 2 Pt 3:9, John 3.16, Is 53:3-5, Col 2:14, Rom 3:26)

4. Response

Obviously this offer is not based on our merit – we don't deserve such treatment and certainly can't earn it through trying to be good. Rather it is on offer because God is good and gracious and generous.

Yet, as with all gifts, it must be opened if you want to benefit from it. Yet amazingly there are people who don't want this gift even though it is the only way to be saved and to live again. These foolish people prefer to carry on living the way they are, sinning and being selfish. They don't want to come to God and ask for His forgiveness and start living in a way that is pleasing to Him.

As they reject God, He therefore rejects them. It is their choice not His. He wants everyone to be saved and live with Him eternally. But if people choose differently He respects their choice.

I have made my choice, what about you? Your decision determines your destiny. Here's the Good News - if right now you ask Jesus to come into your heart and be Saviour and Lord of your life, He will give you a new start and a new heart right now. The Bible promises us forgiveness from the past, new life for today and hope for the future. It's fantastic, never has there been such a wonderful gift on offer. Would you like to pray and talk to God right now?

(See Eph 3:8-9, Deut 30:19, 1John 5:12, John 10:10)

PARTNERSHIP Principles

"Give me one hundred preachers who fear nothing but sin and desire nothing but God, and I care not whether they be clergymen or laymen, they alone will shake the gates of Hell and set up the kingdom of Heaven upon Earth."

John Wesley

1st **PARTNERSHIP PRINCIPLE:**
Teamwork makes the dream work

"Go it alone"; "Be your own boss"; "Do it yourself"; are all cries of the modern individualistic world in which we live. But as the story below indicates not partnering with others can seriously undermine your productivity let alone your health.

There was a brick layer who tried to move 250 kilos of bricks from the top of a 4 story building to the ground below. This would have been a relatively simply job for a team to do but this brick layer tried to do it alone. Later, on an insurance claim form, he explained what happened:

"It would have taken too long to carry the bricks down by hand, so I decided to put them in a barrel and lower them by a pulley which I had fastened to the top of the building. After tying the rope securely at the ground level, I then went up to the top of the building. I fastened the rope around the barrel, loaded it with bricks, and swung it out over the pavement for the descent.
Then I went down to the pavement and untied the rope, holding it securely to guide the barrel down slowly. But, since I way only 70 kilos, the 250 kilos of load jerked me from the ground so fast that I didn't have time to think of letting go of the rope. And as I passed between the second and third floors, I met the barrel coming down. This accounts for the bruises and lacerations on my upper body.
I held tightly to the rope until I reached the top, where my hand became jammed in the pulley. This accounts for my broken thumb. At the same time, however, the barrel hit the pavement with a bang and the bottom fell

out. With the weight of the bricks gone, the barrel weighed only about 20 kilos. Thus, my 70 kilo body began a swift descent, and I meet the empty barrel coming up. This accounts for my broken ankle.

Slowed only slightly, I continued the descent and landed on the pile of bricks. This accounts for my sprained back and broken collarbone.

At this point, I lost my presence of mind completely and let go of the rope. And the empty barrel came crashing down on me. This accounts for my head injuries.

As for the last question on the form, 'what would you do if the same situation arose again?' Please be advised that I will never again try to do the job alone."

People produce higher results when working in groups than they do if they were all working individually. In cell-based churches, the cell group consists of group of friends who constantly motivate one another to achieve their growth targets and to invite others to participate. Whereas in programme-based churches, evangelism is normally only engaged when there is a special event organised by the leaders.

Science proves that power is increased through synergy (the sum of the whole is greater than the sum of the parts). For example one horse can pull a certain weight but two horses can pull more than double that weight.

"Five of you shall chase a hundred, and a hundred of you shall put ten thousand to flight;" (Lev 26:8)

If a snowflake falls on your face it will melt. But if enough snowflakes fall together, they can stop traffic! Individually they may be weak, but working together they are a mighty force.

"Behold, how good and how pleasant it is for brethren to dwell together in unity! …For there the Lord commanded the blessing – Life forevermore" (Ps 133:1, 3)

Partnership is the key to achieving much bigger goals. Teamwork makes the dream work!

2ND **PARTNERSHIP** PRINCIPLE:
EVERY MEMBER IS A MINISTER

"Any method of evangelism is good as long as God is in it"
Charles Spurgeon

One of the triumphs of the Protestant Reformation, led by Martin Luther and others, was the revival of the New Testament teaching of the universal priesthood of the believer or, in other words, a Church in which every member is a minister.

"But you are a chosen generation, a royal priesthood, a holy nation, His own special people, that you may proclaim the praises of Him who called you out of darkness into His marvellous light;" (1 Pt 2:9)

As with the high priests of ancient Israel, our responsibility is to talk to God on behalf of men and to talk to men on behalf of God. We must fulfil both functions in order to fulfil our role as royal priesthood here on earth.

Traditional churches generally rely on a missions departments or a select group of "evangelists" to win new people to Christ. I believe that this outreach philosophy has seriously crippled the growth rate of the church.

Evangelism is a corporate responsibility that belongs to each member of the body of Christ. Churches with missions departments send a message to the other church departments, that soul-winning is their area of responsibility and expertise. The downside of this is that other members then feel they have no need of reaching out. "Leave it to the specialists" they think!

The primary function of the Evangelist, as stated in Ephesians 4:11-13, is to equip the body to evangelise. Sure he or she is a person who is gifted in the area of winning souls, but their primary responsibility is to train others to do the work of evangelism.

Many churches have taught their members to specialise in the area of their gifting, but not to focus on their divine purpose. "I am called to be a worshipper", says one. "My gifting is teaching", says another. "I like to intercede", says a third person. Yet all of us are called to bear fruit (John 15:8) and to be "fruitful, multiply and fill the earth" with spiritual children (Gn 1:28)

"...if some are evangelists then is it their job to preach the gospel and be responsible for the work of evangelism rather than every Christian? I remember well when this idea first came to us. It was welcomed with open arms. Everyone immediately discovered they didn't have to bother unless they were 'evangelists'. They were equally certain that none of them was! It was the only time in the history of the country when we were left with no 'evangelists' - (except me, and I had to because I was the Director of the Department of Evangelism!). What a great foolishness it all was."
John Chapman

We should not separate a select few to be "missionaries". In reality we are all called to be missionaries because we are all "men with a mission"! As someone quick-witted put it; "A missionary is not someone who crosses the sea but someone who sees the cross!" Our primary mission fields are not necessarily the deep jungles of Borneo, or whatever other romantic notion we may conjure up, but rather the concrete jungles of the very cities where most of us live.

*We are called to "be" witnesses
not to "do" witnessing.*

"You shall be My witnesses" (Acts 1:8)

Jesus told his disciples that they would become His witnesses after the Holy Spirit had fallen upon them. They would not "do" witnessing but they would "be" witnesses. It would be a lifestyle based on an extraordinary encounter with God that each one would have. They would be so changed that they would not be able to explain their story without testifying of God's transforming power. Ten days after this promise the Spirit fell and the disciples were filled with a passion and zeal to evangelise (Acts 2:1-4). God's river of anointing began to flow through them. They all began to speak in other tongues and to declare the wonderful works of God (Acts 2:11).

*A testimony is a story
that is impossible to explain without God.*

The Spirit's purpose was to empower the Church to proclaim the message of Salvation. Those very disciples who had fled in terror when Jesus had been arrested and who hidden away after his crucifixion for fear of losing their own lives, were now out of the streets preaching to the same people who had previously called for Christ's blood.

Together they were a mighty force. Three thousands souls were saved that day and that was just the beginning. The vast area of Asia Minor was to be impacted by the Gospel in the years following few years (Ac 19:10). The disciples themselves were to be accused of "turning the whole world upside down"! (Ac 17:6) They started in their home city of Jerusalem and then spread out to the neighbouring cities and then to foreign nations.

One spring morning a young boy was walking along the beach when he came to an area where thousands of star fish had been washed up. The previous night there had been a spring tide which had left its debris high up on the sea shore. The hot sun had dried out the star fish and as they could not get back to the sea, they were slowing dying. The little boy picked up a star fish in each hand and strode down to the sea and threw each of them as far as he could back into the water. He then marched back up the beach to the piles of star fish and collected two more and did the same thing again. An hour later an old man approached him. He had been watching the boy from a distance. He had seen the thousands of star fish and the two in the little boy's hands and then said to him, "Son, you are not going to make much of a difference!" The boy threw another star fish into the sea, turned to the old man and replied, "Well I made a difference to that one!"

If church members get personally involved in winning their world, the whole world would be impacted. Yet in the church there seem to be more arm-chair specialists than front-line soldiers! We need "each one to reach one", as the above story demonstrates. We must do what we can do, even if we can't do everything.

3rd PARTNERSHIP PRINCIPLE:
If you know the way you must show the way!

There is no such thing as silent Christianity. Those who have met Jesus are compelled to talk Him. They just cannot keep silent. The news is too good; its transforming power is too great; its promises are too wonderful. If you had just won a million pounds you would struggle to keep the smile off your face and a hop out of your step! If you were physically blind and now could see, you would let the world know. So those who have been saved cannot help but to shout about this amazing God.

Not only is this our normal response to the work of Christ within us, but the Bible teaches that it is our normal responsibility. We are now charged to be salt and light to our generation (Matt 5:13). To hold back the truth makes us culpable in the eyes of God. If you had the cure to cancer, surely it would be your moral and social duty to let sufferers know. So those of us who know "the Way, the Truth, and the Life" (John 14:6) or the true way to Life are duty-bound to let others know.

"You shall be witnesses to Me in Jerusalem, and in all Judea and Samaria, and to the end of the earth." (Acts 1:8)

God's plan for each of us is to firstly witness in our own type of Jerusalem, Judea and Samaria, and even to the ends of the earth.

Firstly we must reach out to our Jerusalem. This implies evangelising our own personal network of family and friends – those people with whom we have much in common.

Secondly we must reach out to our Samaria and Judea. For the Jews, the

Samaritans were people who lived nearby but who had a very different culture. For us today this implies that we must reach out to those who live in our neighbourhoods but with whom we have less in common - for instance people from different cultural, financial or social groups.

Finally we must go the ends of the earth. This implies that we must reach out to strangers and foreigners - those who live in different cities and nations. God wants us to shout about this great news in every nation of the earth. Yet one preacher wisely observed; "In the West we talk about the second coming of Christ whilst in many nations they have not even heard of the first coming!"

We need to be a people that are disposed to leave behind the familiar comforts of our own culture and environment and go to other cities and nations to start cell groups and plant churches. However, if you do decide to travel to other places to win the Lost, please first prove yourself faithful on your home turf. Some people constantly dream of ministering in foreign nations but do little to win their own.

Start with your own house and be fruitful in your home church and then, the leaders will recognise your maturity and ability and delight in sending you to more distant fields.

Some are called and some are sent,
but others bought a microphone and went!

When I converted, I was living in Australia, working for an international company. I immediately witnessed to all my work colleagues and my friends with whom I played rugby and socialised. Shortly afterwards on a long vacation back to the UK, I organised to meet with all my family members, often individually, in order to tell them how I had converted and encourage them to do the same. I then went through my UK address book and met up with many of my friends from school and university days. As I had friends in other countries, I either arranged to meet them when I was next in their countries (such as those in Singapore and Hong Kong) or I wrote detailed letters to them. For others I recorded my conversion story on cassette tape and sent it to them.

When I arrived to work in the Philippines I started a Bible study group during the lunch hour at the business head office. Each month we would have an outreach meeting to which we invited our colleagues. Likewise I started a cell group in my home. This became a thoroughly multi-cultural and mixed group where maids and cleaners joined together with ex-patriot businessmen to worship God and study His word. Shortly afterwards a number of local pastors asked me to come and preach in outdoor evangelistic rallies that they were holding downtown or in the surrounding villages. This was the beginning of my public ministry.

The responsibility of every new convert is to reach to those they know. Having done this it is our responsibility to reach out beyond our own circles of relationships.

Go public and house to house

"You know, **from the first day** that I came to Asia, in what manner I always lived among you, serving the Lord with all humility, with many tears and trials which happened to me by the plotting of the Jews; how **I kept back nothing** that was helpful, but proclaimed it to you, and taught you **publicly and from house to house,** testifying to Jews, and also to Greeks, repentance toward God and faith toward our Lord Jesus Christ. …Therefore I testify to you this day that I am innocent of the blood of **all men**. For I have not shunned to declare to you the whole counsel of God. (Acts 20:18-23, 27-28 Emphasis mine)

The prophet Ezekiel emphasises the responsibility of each believer to reach out to save the life of his fellow man:
"Now it came to pass at the end of seven days that the word of the Lord came to me, saying," Son of man, I have made you a watchman for the house of Israel; therefore hear a word from My mouth, and give them warning from Me: When I say to the wicked, You shall surely die, and you give him no warning, nor speak to warn the wicked from his wicked way, to save his life, that same wicked man shall die in his iniquity; but his blood I

will require at your hand. Yet, if you warn the wicked, and he does not turn from his wickedness, nor from his wicked way, he shall die in his iniquity; but you have delivered your soul." (Ez 3:16-19)

The Apostle Paul seemed to have been personally driven by Ezekiel's words. In his desire to be approved by God, Paul was careful to take every opportunity to preach the full counsel of God to those around him – no matter the cost.

"And see, now I go bound in the spirit to Jerusalem, not knowing the things that will happen to me there, except that the Holy Spirit testifies in every city, saying that chains and tribulations await me. But none of these things move me; nor do I count my life dear to myself, so that I may finish my race with joy, and the ministry which I received from the Lord Jesus, to testify to the gospel of the grace of God." (Acts 20:22-24)

Likewise in his desire to present his disciples perfect before Christ, Paul instructed them to constantly reach out for Christ.

"I charge you therefore before God and the Lord Jesus Christ, who will judge the living and the dead at His appearing and His kingdom: **Preach the word! Be ready in season and out of season.** …But you be watchful in all things, endure afflictions, **do the work of an evangelist, fulfil your ministry."** (2 Tim 4:1-2, 5 Emphasis mine)

Without preaching there can be no salvation. How can people believe unless they hear the Good News of Christ? Sadly the Church has been drastically underperforming, like a four cylinder car motor running on only one cylinder. Most traditional churches leave the preaching to the minister and the witnessing to a specialised few.

Satan's task of destroying mankind (John 10:10) has been made infinitely easier by the absence of anyone to stand up and confront him. It is the Gospel that is the power of God to Salvation (Rom 1:18). The Gospel releases God's power and conquers the work of the enemy. The Church has been fully equipped with weapons of warfare to destroy the strongholds of the enemy. We've got the power! Yet we need to use it. God is waiting for a generation of champions to rise up and take responsibility for the situation on planet earth.

In many places and cases the battle still rages, the enemy still rules, and wickedness still reigns! No wonder God cried out to Isaiah; "Whom shall I send, And who will go for us?" (Is 6:8). No wonder holy indignation burned in the heart of David as he saw Goliath threatening to subjugate God's people to oppressive rule; "Is there not a cause?" (1Sm 17:29). No wonder the fire smoldered inside of Jeremiah until he could be silent no more; "But His word was in my heart like a burning fire shut up in my bones; I was weary of holding it back, and I could not." (Jer 20:9). Surely we all, like Isaiah, must respond, "Here am I! Send me." (Is 6:8).

The battle of our mouths
determines the battle for their minds

If it is the Holy Spirit's plan to for us to preach, then you can be sure it is the devil's plan for us to be silent. The battle is for the mouth. Silent Christians are those who have been captured and disarmed by the enemy. What Satan fears most is many voices proclaiming the Good News.

The kingdom of darkness survives by keeping people locked up in a prison of deception. People who are deceived do not know that they are deceived! They can and will only gain perception of their deception when the light of truth is shined upon them. Only truth can remove a lie.

When people think differently they will live differently. Repentance literally means "to think again". In other words to understand there is a different life to lead and to determine to walk in that path. If there were many voices in every part of society exposing Satan's lies and proclaiming God's truth, a generation could be won at speed.

Only by partnering in this purpose will this become a reality. God's plan is for our many mouths to proclaim one message. Like a coordinated choir we are to be many voices sounding as one voice!

PROVISION Principles

"Life's most persistent and urgent question is 'What are we doing for others?'"
Martin Luther King Jr

It is one thing to pray for the salvation of people, it is another thing to put everything at your disposal into winning them. As one preacher said "We need to put feet to our prayers". There are three main areas that we should offer to God if we are truly committed to winning the Lost. They are:

Time
Talents
Treasures

In England we use plugs with three prongs for all our electrical appliances. A light will only function if it is connected to the main power supply. It is one thing to have power in the house, it is another to have that power flowing through the appliances – they need to be connected. Likewise there is power in the Church. The Holy Spirit is resident here on earth. But unless we plug into Him by offering the three connectors - time, talents and treasures – His power is not able to flow through us.

People who hold back any of these three things maybe members of the church but they are not connected to the body of Christ in a real sense. As the life of God is not flowing through them, they can bear no fruit.

It has been said that God does not use those who are most capable but rather those who are most available. The power of God rests upon people who are committed to God, not just in words, but in actions; not just in praying but also in paying! Ultimately those who pay the price become most valuable to the Lord. They become His champion soul-winners. They become the fathers to generations of spiritual sons.

1st PROVISION Principle:
Believers must input their time.

"Do all the good you can, to all you the people you can, in all the ways you can, as long as you can"
DL Moody

People are won to the Lord through relationships. (Even great evangelists such as Billy Graham concede that the success of their crusades is based on believers bringing loved ones to the event.) People are constantly searching for true friends upon whom they can count. When they find someone trustworthy they are able to open up their hearts and hurts and be ministered to.

It takes time to build a relationship. Trust does not spring up overnight. There are no short cuts. People talk about quality time being as good as or better than quantity time. They say that it does not matter how much time you give but how effectively you use the time. I believe this is only a half-truth. Sure we need to be effective with our time but if you only give short amounts of time to relationships they are rarely fruitful. Somebody once said that true love is spelt T-I-M-E. You cannot love without giving your time.

It is impossible to develop our relationship with God without spending time in prayer and communion with Him. Short prayers before meals or bed are hardly sufficient to build a strong relationship. You would have problems in your marriage if you only spoke to your wife thirty seconds before meals and before bed!

People don't care how much you know until they know how much your care.

When you think about it time is the most precious asset on earth. Each day we are given 24 hours or 1440 minutes or 86,400 seconds. This time can never be replaced in your life. It is spent for ever. Everyday you are one step closer to your day of departure from earth.

Imagine if a billionaire put £86,400 pounds into your bank account every morning but at night he removes whatever was not spent. You would busy yourself using every penny everyday. We have life, in the form of time, put into our accounts everyday by God. We should similarly busy ourselves spending it wisely, for those minutes and seconds will never be repeated again.

Time is precious because it can be exchanged for anything in life. You can use it to make money, play sports, or relax. Imagine if you use some of this precious substance of time for the well-being of others. What a noble sacrifice! You could have used it for your own pleasure or gain but you put other peoples' needs in a higher place than yours. It is no wonder that this touches the hearts of others.

Consumer Christians only give the amount of time necessary to be a participant in church life. They reckon that by giving an hour mid-week and a couple of hours at the weekend that they have given much to the service of God. Really they have a client mentality – they are not there to give but only to receive. This type of Christian normally complains about so many church meetings; yet don't think twice about meeting with the television for hours every week!

On the other hand Producer Christians spend their time visiting people in the week, planning their cell groups, and inviting and then bringing their friends to their meetings. They linger longer than others after services in order to meet people's needs, answer questions and serve the body of Christ. They live a life of service not because they are obliged to by the pastor but rather because they want to express their gratitude to God by serving Him and His people.

Learn to linger longer!

When Moses died, Joshua was appointed as the next leader of Israel. He was not Moses' son but he became his natural successor. Why was this? It is true that he was a great warrior and inspirational leader. He was also a man of faith as exemplified when he and Caleb were the only two spies who believed that Israel was able to conquer the land of Canaan. But where did such faith and leadership capacity come from? I believe because he lingered longer than anyone else in the in the presence of the Lord in the tabernacle.

There is a great reward to giving more time to God. If you stand before God you will be able to stand before men. If you dedicate more time to God and His work, your life becomes more valuable to Him.

Lingering longer is the key to standing stronger! Time is the key to many situations. Too many of us quit too soon; if we would only keep on going we would see the results to our labours. A pregnant woman needs to complete her term before her baby can be born. Yet often we are guilty of aborting our efforts to bringing spiritual children into the world by giving up when the going gets tough or requires too much time.

A good exercise is to monitor how much time you give to the Lord each week. How much time do you give outside of service times? Would it be too much to ask to give just one hour of your day? Why not try setting aside specific times each week to telephone your network of friends, to visit their houses, or to help out if they are in need? The results would be immediate.

The church cannot grow if the members do not commit their time. Yet the converse is true as well. If members commit more time the churches tend to grow. Ultimately our time here on earth is given to us to bring glory to God. We have only one life and can never rewind the clock. The graveyards are full of people who died with regrets that they could have done more. The ground is full of unfulfilled dreams! Let us have the same fervour to give our time to God as the Wesley brothers had in the 18th Century. Charles Wesley said to his older brother John, "Brother, let us pray that when we get to heaven that we would not look back and see that we have wasted even two minutes of our time on earth".

These brothers were concerned about wasting a couple of minutes! Help

Lord! Most of us have wasted months and years! It is not that we should not rest and relax or take breaks and holidays; but what we must do is break out of the spirit of lethargy and passivity when it is time to be in action.

2ND PROVISION PRINCIPLE:
Believers must involve their talents.

NATURAL TALENTS:

In many parts of the West the work of the ministry has, in the eyes of the world, become a second rate job occupation. Parents hope that their children will become doctors or lawyers or businessmen, but rarely pastors or church leaders.

I remember as an eight year old boy I had a custom to pray by the side of my bed each evening. On one occasion my mother came in to my room and found me kneeling in prayer. She sat down next to me and with tears in her eyes said, "Honey, please don't become a monk when you grow up!"

My mother's reaction at the time was typical of the post-modern mentality towards the ministry (whilst also being somewhat illogical in that praying does not necessarily lead to a monastic lifestyle!). The thinking is that church work really is not a "proper job"; and that church involvement should be limited to Sunday services or weddings and funerals!

In contrast to the West many churches in Latin America, Africa and Asia have young men queuing up to be in full time ministry. For instance there are businessmen, farmers, doctors, policemen, and accountants who have stopped working in the secular world in order to give more time to the work of the ministry.

Many western churches are full of highly educated and professional people who, in the secular world, are responsible for large sums of money or large groups of people. Yet often when they come to church the only responsibility they have is to make the tea or greet people at the door. This is all well and good but surely the church would benefit if they could be more involved in leadership training, managing cell groups, coaching new leaders etc.

Many churches limit themselves and the people to get involved because their plans are too small. Put an audacious plan before a talented person and he rises to the challenge and wants to be involved. But ask him or her to manage a second hand hat sale to restore the church roof, and he is heading for the door! Big thinking attracts big thinkers. Big vision attracts big donors.

Outreach and discipleship is dependant on an efficient, well-managed organisational structure. Many churches suffer from stunted growth not because their members are not spiritually gifted or anointed; but rather because the spiritual dimension is not adequately supported by a administrative structure.

Churches should be run efficiently and effectively as any serious CEO or MD would run their company. Obviously church vision and values are different. It is not our goal to make a financial profit. It is our goal to win our generation for Jesus. However, we need to be professional as well as spiritual if we are to achieve these goals. And to this end we need people to willingly involve their talents.

SUPERNATUTAL TALENTS:

The Gifts of the Spirit

Supernatural or divine talents are the gifts of the Spirit that are given to the members of the church. The nine gifts can be divided into three groups of three.

THE REVELATORY GIFTS: Word of Wisdom, Word of Knowledge, Discerning of spirits.
THE POWER GIFTS: Gift of Faith, Healings, Miracles.
THE SPOKEN GIFTS: Prophesy, Tongues, Interpretation of tongues.

The Parable of the unfaithful servant in Matthew Chapter 25 is concerned with what believers do with their spiritual talents. In short, the servant who buries his gift is strictly judged by the Lord. God requires us to be faithful in all we have by employing what we have for the benefit of others.

So how is it possible for every member to exercise the gifts of the Spirit? Not many people can minister in a Sunday service – only the pastor, the worship team and any others who lead the meeting. However, cell groups give room for every member to be involved ministering to one another on a regular basis.

These smaller meetings should never be mini-Sunday services where only one brother preaches a long message and the others simply listen and learn. Cell group leaders should be able to introduce and lead a discussion involving all of the members. Likewise, he or she is to give the others space to prophesy, or give words of wisdom and knowledge, as well as the other gifts of the Spirit.

Cell groups provide the environment for all church members to be exercising their spiritual gifts.

Leaders who do not set up a structure and culture in which members can exercise their talents are in reality limiting the growth of the church and robbing their flock of future rewards. If we are to be judged for not using our talents, you can be sure also that the Christian leader will be judged for not using his members in the ministry!

The operation of Spiritual talents is vital for growth. The Apostle Paul was keen that everyone sought the Lord eagerly to be used in this area (1 Co 14:1) as he realised the importance of the gifts to grow his churches.

The Acts of the Spirit

The Book of Acts is an abbreviation for The Book of the Acts of the Apostles. However, it is actually a book containing the Acts of the Holy Spirit in those apostles. A study of this book reveals that the mass conversions of souls occurred after there was some sort of move of the Holy Spirit.

In Acts Chapter two the 120 disciples were filled with the Spirit, spoke in other languages and prophesied and, as a result, 3000 people converted to Christ. Equipped with these supernatural gifts they profoundly convicted their listeners to the point that they cried out: "What must we do to be saved?" (The Baptism of the Holy Spirit released these giftings within the disciples – hence the baptism is not a goal in itself but a gateway to the supernatural gifts of the Spirit.) When these gifts are in action, the harvest is easily reaped.

> *The Baptism of the Holy Spirit is not a goal in itself but actually a gateway to the supernatural gifts of the Spirit.*

In Acts Chapter three Peter, through the gifts of faith and miracles, commanded a lame man to rise up and walk. The man arose and entered the temple "walking, leaping and praising God" to the amazement of the crowd. Peter preached once more and the number of believers increased to 5000 (Acts 4:4).

In Acts Chapter five, through the discernment of spirits, Peter realised that Ananias and Sapphira, had lied to God concerning their offering. Their immediate deaths understandably brought great fear upon the people. Through such signs and wonders many others were added to the church (Acts 5:12-14).

In every chapter of the book of Acts we can read how the gifts of the Spirit are used constantly and bring immediate results. The book itself is a résumé of the activities of a number of the Apostles, yet almost every chapter list the operation of spiritual gifts.

Finally in Acts chapter twenty-eight, the last chapter, Paul, through the gift of healing, laid his hand on the leading citizen of Malta and healed him of fever and dysentery. This led all the other sick on the island to come to him and be cured. The Gospel impacted the whole island. The locals had first thought Paul to be a murderer but quickly changed their minds and welcomed him as a life-saver! A local revival has broken out as a result of these gifts in action.

Imagine if each member of the church was flowing in the gifts of the Spirit. Imagine the power and effect that our cell groups would have if every week wonderful miracles were happening from house to house in our cities.

On a recent Encounter weekend in Goiania, Brazil, I was with a youth pastor who encouraged every member of his team to give a word of knowledge about the sicknesses of the participants. 37 people responded to those words and were instantly healed. The Holy Spirit had revealed every sickness to the ministry team.

All believers have been given talents as the Spirits wills (1 Co 12:7, 11). Therefore all must be encouraged to use them regularly. Sadly in many churches, these spiritual talents are buried away. If these talents are the keys to unlock the hearts of the lost, it is no wonder that the Lord both rewards and chastises his stewards according to how they use their talents

3rd PROVISION PRINCIPLE:
Believers must invest their treasures.

Revival has a cost. You can't expect to give birth to children and it not cost you. My wife recently gave birth to our third son. With every pregnancy there is a list of items to be paid - ultra-sound scans, medical check-ups, food supplements, etc. Then there is the birth itself and the hospital bills. After which the long list of baby necessities is added to our weekly shopping list – nappies, wipes, powdered-milk, clothes, etc.

It is not cheap to give birth to a child but my God it is worth it! The blessings far outweigh the burdens! Winning souls and training them to be disciples is a costly process too. The list could include - praying for them, visiting them, helping them organise their lives, buying them spiritual material, or paying for them to go on Encounter weekends etc. But my Lord, when that person gets saved and filled with the Holy Spirit, and matures into a man or woman of God, you forget the expense. Why? Because it was more than worth it. I can think of no greater investment.

Some years ago I held a number of evangelistic events in the Philippines with a YWAM drama team. They would act out a song by Ray Boltz called "Thank you for giving to the Lord". In the song a believer arrives in heaven and finds a long line of people there waiting to greet him whom he had never seen before. These people tell him that they are there as a result of him giving funds to a missionary so that he could travel and preach to them.

> *"Today some Christians spend more money on dog food than on missions!"*
> Leonard Ravenhill

There is a story that once upon a time a one-pound coin met a fifty-pound note. The coin said to the note; "It's great to meet you. Where have you been all your life?" The fifty-pound note replied, "I've been in the casinos, in the bars, in the theatres, in the restaurants and in the finest places on earth!" The fifty-pound note then returned the same question to the coin. "What about you, where have you been?" The one-pound coin said gloomily, "For me it's been the same old thing, week in, week out - church, church, church!"

> *Many people buy things they don't need,*
> *with money they don't have*
> *to impress people they don't like!*

When we spend money on ourselves we hardly think about it but when we spend it on others or give it in tithes and offerings we count every penny! In England we have a picture of the Queen on our notes. We say that some people squeeze their notes so tight that the Queen begins to cry!

In the Kingdom of God it is the generous ones who are the most fruitful. God's blessing is upon them. Why? Because if God has control of your check book then He certainly has control of your heart. In other words He will direct you and minister through you. If we are faithful with unrighteous mammon then God gives us the true riches of the Kingdom of heaven which is the power of the Holy Spirit (Luke 16:11).

Somebody once said, "But pastor, the Gospel is free?" I replied: "True, but, like water, it costs something to pump it to people". In a world that is bent on money-making and pleasure-seeking, God is looking to move through a people who are willing to give joyfully to the work of reaching out to save others.

Money is like manure. If you pile it up it smells.
But if you spread it around, you can encourage things to grow.

Let us spend and be spent in the work of reaching the lost in any way we can. As John Wesley said, "Money is food for the hungry, clothes for the naked, medicine for the sick." For this reason master your money but never let your money master you. Be generous with your earthly treasures and you will win heavenly treasures.

"If a person gets his attitude straight about money, it will help straighten out almost every other area of his life."

Billy Graham

PASSION PRINCIPLES

"Give me the love that leads the way,
The faith that nothing can dismay,
The hope no disappointments tire,
The passion that will burn like fire,
Let me not sink to be a clod:
Make me Thy fuel, Flame of God."

Amy Carmichael

"If sinners be damned, at least let them leap to hell over our bodies. And if they perish, let them perish with our arms about their knees, imploring them to stay. If hell must be filled, at least let it be filled in the teeth of our exertions, and let not one go there unwarned and unprayed for."

Charles Spurgeon

1st PASSION PRINCIPLE:
PASSIONATE PEOPLE OVERCOME THE OBSTACLES THAT CAUSE DISPASSIONATE PEOPLE TO GIVE UP

In Mel Gibson's film "The passion of Christ", a view of the determination of the son of God to complete His earthly objective comes across in dramatic reality. Christ rejects any distraction or temptation to choose an easier path. His Gethsemane prayer reveals His passionate intent: "O My Father, if it possible, let this cup pass from Me; nevertheless, not as I will, but as You will." (Matt 26:39). He did not defend Himself in front of Pontius Pilate and He refused to talk to Herod. He did not contradict the High Priests or refute their contrived accusations. (It is probable that such a defence would have made little difference.) Jesus' earthly purpose was to be crucified for the sins of the world. He, who knew no sin, was to become Sin on our behalf, that we might become the righteousness of God (2 Cor 5:21). He was to exact a divine exchange - our sinfulness for His righteousness. His purpose was clear but, my friends, it took every ounce of His passion to achieve it.

Jesus is our supreme example and the Bible teaches that we should look to Him in order to overcome the difficult circumstances that arise in life:

"looking unto Jesus, the author and finisher of our faith, who for the joy that was set before Him endured the cross, despising the shame, and has sat down at the right hand of the throne of God. For consider Him who endured such hostility from sinners against Himself, lest you become weary and discouraged in your souls." (Hebrews 12:2-3)

Passion is the pre-requisite in fulfilling God's purposes. His plans cannot be accomplished by the faint-hearted or the weak-willed. Passion is the driving force that takes a man past the obstacles that lie in his way and on to victory. Christ-like passion comes alive in you when you discover the thing you live for is worth dying for!

> *"I will open Africa to the gospel or die trying."*
> Missionary Rowland Bingham

The Apostle Paul's passion reflected his master.

And see, now I go bound in the spirit to Jerusalem, not knowing the things that will happen to me there, except that the Holy Spirit testifies in every city, saying that chains and tribulations await me. But none of these things move me; nor do I count my life dear to myself, so that I may finish my race with joy, and the ministry, which I received from the Lord Jesus, to testify to the gospel of the grace of God. (Acts 20:22-24)

For to me, to live is Christ, and to die is gain." (Phil 1:21)

For I am already being poured out as a drink offering, and the time of my departure is at hand. I have fought the good fight, I have finished the race, I have kept the faith. Finally, there is laid up for me the crown of righteousness, which the Lord, the righteous Judge, will give to me on that Day, and not to me only but also to all who have loved His appearing." (1 Ti 4:6-8)

Paul finished his race and won his crown. He fathered thousands of spiritual children; he birthed countless churches; he laid down a firm foundation of doctrine for his disciples; he raised a new generation of leaders; and he kept his heart pure and his relationship intimate with the Lord in the process. We would do well to imitate his passion as he imitated Christ's (1Co 11:1).

"I have but one passion - it is He, it is He alone. The world is the field and the field is the world; and henceforth that country shall be my home where I can be most used in winning souls for Christ."
Count Zinzindorf

"A great leader's courage to fulfil his vision comes from passion, not position."
John Maxwell

You never achieve your goals in life unless you are passionate. You must come to the place where you let passion explode within you. A lack of passion signifies a lack of desire. You just don't want it enough. Many people do not receive or achieve for the simple reason that they are not fervent enough for their goals. God waits to see who is serious about doing business in the kingdom of heaven. "Draw near to God and He will draw near to you." (James 4:8). You have to press into a place with an attitude that says "Lord if you do not touch me right now, then I am going to come up there and touch you!" Or as Jacob said to the angel of the Lord when he wrestled with Him: "I will not let you go unless You bless me." (Gen 32:26)

Be done with half-hearted prayers and half-hearted witnessing. Go for it with all your heart. Tear up the heavenly realms. Pull down the strongholds. Shout out the victory. Release the power of God on your life!

There is no reward for a lazy man. There is no harvest for the sluggard. There is no productivity without passion.

"The lazy man will not plough because of winter; He will beg during harvest and have nothing" (Pr 20:4)

To be a great soul winner, you must have a passion for souls. Some people tell me that they are so passionate for the Lord, but they spend little effort trying to win others. I believe that if you are passionate for the Lord you will be passionate for the things that He is passionate about. If He left the glory and comfort of heaven to come to a sin-stricken world to save lost sinners, then we too should be zealously involved in the Father's business of seeking and saving that which is lost.

Sure, it is not an easy path. Jesus never promised it would be. You will be misunderstood and rejected by some. Yet it is a worthwhile path, as you will experience when you lead someone to salvation and start to generate your own spiritual children. Jesus said; "Straight is the gate and difficult is the way" but it leads to LIFE (Matt 7:13-14). Passion is the power that drives you on through the hard times. If you feel like you are going throw hell, then don't stop! Let passion push you on.

"God loves with a great love the man whose heart is bursting with a passion for the impossible."

William Booth

Some believers are easily discouraged, especially when people don't respond to their invitations to receive Christ. But the passionate person pushes on. Ultimately he is serving God not man. This is what thrills him most. Therefore whether people respond or not is not his business. Rather it is his business to be a faithful witness. He knows that it is the Lord who gives the increase (1Co 3:7). No price is too high for him to pay, no distance too far to travel, no situation too uncomfortable, in the hope of winning one soul for Christ.

There is a story of a prisoner in England many years ago who was condemned to die by hanging. Before he was placed in the gallows with the rope around his neck, it was tradition for a priest to read out certain scriptures to the condemned. The priest read from the Bible in a lacklustre manner and then turned to leave without prayer. On hearing these scriptures for the first time the prisoner exclaimed: "I had not known about the destiny of men's souls who die without Christ, why has it taken until now for someone to tell me this truth? And why do those who tell this message do so with such little passion? If England were covered in broken glass from north to south I would crawl over it all on my hands and knees just to warn just one man his need to turn to Christ."

If a house was on fire would you jump into action to save those inside? If a train was heading towards a broken bridge and you could call ahead to stop it, would you respond with urgency? Of course! Friends the situation demands a passionate response. Our world is heading for destruction. There is only one way of escape – the Gospel of the Lord Jesus is the power of God to save. If you were on a plane that was going to crash, you would not just quietly recommend that passengers put on parachutes and jump out, you would passionately persuade people! We are not simply offering people a better life-style or standard of living. We are not simply offering peace, joy and prosperity. We are primarily offering a way of escape from certain death and a Christless eternity.

Could a mariner sit idle if he heard the drowning cry? Could a doctor sit in comfort and just let his patients die? Could a fireman sit idle, let men burn and give no hand? Can you sit at ease in Zion with the world around you damned?
Leonard Ravenhill

Lord, give us passion to conquer our fears and phobias, that we might rescue people from the jaws of hell, that we might plunder hell and populate heaven!

2ND **PASSION** PRINCIPLE:
VISION IS THE CATALYST OF PASSION.

"If God is with you, then make your plans big"
Charles Spurgeon

Some people are just not passionate because their vision for life is simply too small. God can't be in it because He is involved in great works. As

Spurgeon once said; "If God is with you, then make your plans big". Passion is derived from your vision for life. You need to be something that gets you out of bed with bounce in the mornings? What is your driving force? Can you see the white and ripened harvest fields all around you that are waiting for labourers (John 4:35)? Can you hear the cry of the sick, the sad and the suffering?

> *"Oh dear, I couldn't say that my church is alive and I wouldn't want to call it dead. I guess it's just walking in its sleep!"*
>
> A church member

David Wilkerson, the founder and pastor of the Times Square Church in New York, has been a model of unceasing passion for the lost since the start of his inner-city ministry to drug gangs in the 1960's. He says that whenever he feels his passion begin to dwindle, he goes for a long walk through the ghettoes of New York. He watches the kids on the streets shooting up, he listens to the cursing and swearing coming from the tower-blocks, and he sees the squalor and sinful mentality that is destroying countless lives and families. By the time he returns back home, he is pumped with passion again. Why? Because God has renewed his vision. He has seen the desperate state of people without Christ. He has remembered that the church is the only hope for people in this life and the next.

> *"The 3.5 billion unreached people on earth would form a single file line that would stretch around the equator 25 times! Can you picture 25 lines of Christless people, trampling endlessly toward hell? Let that vision stay with you day and night."*
>
> Larry Stockstill

You are called to be productive. You are to be a father of nations. There are spiritual children in your spiritual loins. Let the passion of Christ in you manifest. Give Him full sway in your life. Do not let a foolish thing like laziness steal this amazing abundant life that Christ has for you. Listen to the remorseful words of the prophet Jeremiah when he considered the state of his own nation.

"The harvest is past, the summer is over and we are not saved." (Jer 8:20)

In light of the revelation that we have an eternity of glory ahead of us, to be lukewarm now is a tragedy. Lukewarm praise, lukewarm prayers and lukewarm preaching are lamentable. It is better not to do a thing than to do it in a lukewarm manner. All of what we do should either be burning hot or refreshingly cold (Rev 3:16). Spurgeon would pray that his disciples would not just have a vision of heaven but a vision of hell. To have an image of the terrible torments of hell burned into your consciousness will act as a driving force in your determination to win the Lost.

"Jehovah Witnesses don't believe in hell and neither do most Christians!"
Leonard Ravenhill

Lamentably today many Christians rarely touch upon the subject of hell. Yet Jesus spoke about it more than heaven and more than love. In correcting our children, earthly fathers tell them they will be punished if they continue to break the rules. No wonder that Spurgeon also taught his disciples to preach both heaven and hell; and to let their faces shine when they spoke of heaven but to weep profusely when they spoke of hell.

In contrast to a lukewarm posture, passionate prayers break through in the spirit world. Passionate preaching melts the hardest hearts. Passionate praise releases the presence of God.

"By the time the average Christian gets his temperature up to normal, everybody thinks he has a fever!"
Watchman Nee

The promises of winning this generation for Christ depend upon your passion. God promised Joshua that, wherever the soles of his feet would tread, He would give the land to the children of Israel as their inheritance. Yet immediately afterwards God exhorted him saying to him three times "Be strong and of good courage" (Joshua 1:1-9). So let me say something similar to you; "GO FOR IT! YOU CAN DO IT! YOU ARE A CHAMPION SOUL WINNER! GOD HAS A GREAT PLAN FOR YOU! PEOPLE ARE WAITING FOR YOU TO MINISTER TO THEM! JUST BE

REALLY BOLD AND COURAGEOUS AND YOU WILL SEE GOD MOVE!"

No matter how young or how old, no matter the length of time in the faith, if your heart-felt desire is to see His name made famous and honoured around the world, the Holy Spirit will use you powerfully.

3RD PASSION PRINCIPLE:
PASSION ATTRACTS.

Whether it be for good or for evil, passionate people have always attracted others. On the negative side Hitler attracted millions of fellow countrymen to unite with him through his passionate plea for world domination through the Third Reich. On the positive side, Martin Luther King Jr attracted thousands of African-Americans and others to rally with him against social inequality. His passionate dream still burns in the hearts of his adherents. At the time of writing I have just heard of the death of the nature preservationist and television personality Steve Irwin. He attracted millions of viewers world-wide to watch his shows. Why? Because he was passionate about dangerous animals.

With all due respect to those who have done their best to better the earth in which we live, surely there is a purpose of incomparable importance to which we believers must dedicate our lives. This world is passing away, life here on earth is short, and a new heaven and earth is coming, eternal life is one heart-beat away. We must usher as many people as possible into that kingdom. As Evangelist Reinhard Bonnke says, "We must plunder hell and populate heaven!"

> *"I love to live on the brink of eternity."*
> David Brainerd

In contrast, impassionate people repel others. Out of choice few people stick around if the company is boring! Some people complain that nobody visits them, calls them, or follows their lead. In my opinion much of this is due to a fault of passion. If they would only stop blaming others and get passionate about something worthwhile, then others would flock around them.

You'll find your passion is one of your greatest weapons. When people see passion in your eyes they will listen to your words.

In the summer of 1989 I spent my summer holidays travelling with a friend through the USA and Central America. We started our journey in New Orleans, Louisiana. Though we were not Christians we decided to visit a black Pentecostal church on Sunday morning for a cultural experience. (People go to church for the first time for all sorts of reasons!) Us white boys, with our long hair and faded jeans, must have looked quite a sight to the church members who were all dressed in the Sunday best - men in suits, women with hats, even the children we dressed to the nines! The place was immaculate. We were greeted warmly at the door and then ushered into a huge auditorium that sat three thousand or more. Already I was feeling slightly overwhelmed but when we went inside we realised that we were the only whites in the place. The place was packed to the rafters! When the worship music started up the whole room began to move with the beat! The sound was huge. I had never been in a church like that in my life. People were dancing in the aisles, singing at the top of their lungs, shouting out intermittently and hugging one another without the slightest inhibition. For a young conservative Englishman, raised only in very traditional high churches, this was a different world! The pastor got up and preached up a storm. On my left and right people jumped up as he was preaching and hollered "Hallelujah" and "Amen" and "You're preaching my story, preacher!" I sat in a state of semi-shock. I wanted to join them but my own self-consciousness held me back. To cut to the point, I don't remember all that was said and done that day, but one thing always stuck in my mind – their passion! They really believed what they singing and preaching about! This was not the hot-air of emotion but the expression of heart-felt belief. I found myself desperately attracted to that. I wanted the freedom that they had. Deep within I was searching for the real meaning of life – by the look in their eyes they had certainly discovered that! From that day forward I wanted to hear more about Jesus' teachings.

THREE PASSIONS:

1. BE PASSIONATE ABOUT GOD'S PROMISES

Hannah prayed with passion, to the extent that Eli the prophet thought she was drunk, and God healed her barrenness and she gave birth to the great prophet Samuel.

Many people in the body of Christ have never given birth to their own spiritual son. To date they are spiritually sterile. But passionate prayer can cure you of that. Those who pray and praise in times of difficulty reveal great faith and hence release the power of heaven.

"Sing, O barren, you who have not borne! Break forth into singing, and cry aloud, you who have not labored with child: for more are the children of the desolate than the children of the married woman, says the LORD." (Isa 54:1)

2. BE PASSIONATE ABOUT GOD'S PEOPLE

Our love for others is the measure stick of our love for God. It is one thing to tell God how much you love Him during a church service; it is another thing to love God by loving undeserving and unthankful people. Jesus said; "In as much you did it to these the least of my brethren, you did it for Me." (Matt 25:40).

Be passionate for people. Jesus is the friend of sinners. In other words many sinners liked to be around Him. Why? Because He was passionate about helping them to change their lives. It is true that God can't help the person who does not want to change. But many people do want to change – they are waiting to find somebody who can help show them the way.

> *"Carve your name in hearts not in marble"*
> Charles Spurgeon

If it is the devil's aim to "steal, kill and destroy" people's lives, then it must be our aim to replenish, revive, rebuild them!

Somebody once said; "You can't make other people feel important in your presence if you secretly feel that he is a nobody." We need to learn to see people as God sees them.

One day as a young boy, I was waiting at a bus stop when I saw a crumpled dirty piece of paper on the ground. I looked closer and realised that it was a five pound note. So I reached down, picked it up, straightened it out and wiped it off! Later I spent it buying sweets and other school boy delights. I also learned an important lesson - whether the note was clean or dirty, whether it was in my hand or on the floor, its value remained the same.

So too with people! Sadly many have suffered at the hands of others. Many people are still struggling with the injustices that were committed against them as they grew up. Some were used, others abused. Some never received any love or affection from parents, others were pressurised into doing things they did not want only to regret it later and carry the emotional scars. In short they feel they have lost their worth value and been left discarded by the road side of life. But in God's eyes, their value is the same as the person with a fine education, perfect manners, and successful career.

However, in order for their value to be realised, someone else needs to reach down, pick them up, straighten them out and wipe them down. They cannot do this alone. They are waiting for a passer-by who will see worth in them. Such is the nature of the Good Samaritan. Be passionate for people and people will respond to your goodness.

3.   BE PASSIONATE ABOUT GOD'S PLAN

Your life is a gift from God. You are writing the script. You need not be controlled by anyone else. Therefore write an exciting, adventurous script where you are the hero and where you accomplish great things. God's plan for you is as a big as you can make it!

Get passionate about your life – you will only live it once. Live it full. Dream big, because God is big! Talk like a champion, for there is a champion within you. No-one ever was elected Prime Minister or President talking like a loser! God chose for you to be born at such a time as this for a specific purpose. He knew what the world would need and He sent you to provide the answer. God foreknew the problems of your generation and your location and sent you to be the solution. He knows the end from the beginning and therefore planned your coming into the world with a divine purpose. You are on a divine mission – to seek and save the Lost, to restore the broken relationships, to heal hurting hearts, to show the true way to life.

Heaven is cheering you on. Heaven's power is at our disposal. Be passionate about the 24 hours that you have today. You will never have them again. Life is for living!

Break free. Don't be a religious robot, chanting out biblical verses like a mantra. Get real. Dare to be yourself. Don't conform to other people's opinions of you. You are bigger than that. Inside of you is the God-given desire to be significant. Release the desire. Realise the dream.

Be passionate about your life. Love it! Live it! You are filling books in heaven with the stories that will last for an eternity.

PERSISTENCE PRINCIPLES

"I am a slow walker but I never walk backwards"
Abraham Lincoln

1st PERSISTENCE PRINCIPLE:
PERSISTENCE BREAKS DOWN RESISTANCE.

Most people are reluctant to embrace new things. They fear the unknown. They fear change. People are especially reluctant to accept new teachings that may challenge their traditions and their lifestyles. However, this does not necessarily mean that they will not accept it or do not want to change. Rather it shows that they are more comfortable with their established thinking and philosophy. The key to helping people through this process is persistence.

"Ride on! Rough-shod if need be, smooth-shod if that will do, but ride on! Ride on over all obstacles, and win the race!"
Charles Dickens

When the unbeliever hears the Gospel he or she enters into a serious spiritual battle. The devil, who has blinded their minds throughout their lives (Eph 2)), has his authority as lord of the person's life challenged. He is not one to give up without a fight. (And I believe he fights so hard because he knows how quickly many Christians desist.)

We must learn to persist in our praying and our preaching. The apostle Paul reasoned daily with people, persuading them concerning the Kingdom of God (Acts 19:8, 28:23). To persuade means not only to present your case but also to refute arguments, expose lies, and reveal the truth. We must not shrink back from the battle at hand.

"And he went into the synagogue, and spoke boldly for the space of three months, disputing and persuading them things concerning the kingdom of

God." (Acts 19:8)

"So when they had appointed him a day, many came to him at his lodging, to whom he explained and solemnly testified of the kingdom of God, persuading them concerning Jesus from both the Law of Moses and the Prophets, from morning till evening." (Acts 28:23)

The power of persistence was wonderfully demonstrated in the following account in the Gospel of Luke. Jesus had been preaching all morning and the disciples had been fishing all night. Jesus had caught a net full of souls but the disciples had a net empty of fish!

"When He had stopped speaking, He said to Simon, "Launch out into the deep and let down your nets for a catch. But Simon answered and said to Him, "Master, we have toiled all night and caught nothing; nevertheless at Your word I will let down the net." And when they had done this, they caught a great number of fish, and their net was breaking. So they signaled to their partners in the other boat to come and help them. And they came and filled both the boats, so that they began to sink. When Simon Peter saw it, he fell down at Jesus' knees, saying, "Depart from me, for I am a sinful man, O Lord" (Luke 5:5-7)

Peter's response was based on experience and expertise. Jesus had told them to throw out their nets, but he had responded by agreeing to put out one net as a way to please Him. He was effectively saying, "Lord, you are a great preacher but you don't know much about fishing. We have been up all night, we know these waters, and if we can't catch fish then nobody can. But because it is you who is asking I will put out a net to test your word." No doubt Peter demonstrated some faith in that he partially obeyed the word of the Lord. However, this was mixed with some unbelief as he lowered down only one net. Yet the results were astounding. There were so many fish that their colleagues had to come and help them pull the net in and even then the boats nearly sank with the weight of fish. Peter recognising his own lack of total faith humbles himself in front of the Lord and exclaims his own sinfulness.

*Persistent people begin their success
where others end in failure.*

The lesson the Lord Jesus taught his disciples on this occasion was two-fold. Firstly they could trust in His word. Whatever He says will come to pass if you believe and act on it. If He says there are fish to be caught then there are fish to be caught. If he says the harvest is white (John 4:35) then the harvest is ripe. We need to believe his Word and go to it.

Secondly that they should never desist, even when all looks lost. He was teaching them that when most people quit, that is the time to continue! Was Jesus interested in starting a fishing business? No! He was training his disciples to be fishers of men. Just as you should not desist in trying again to catch fish, so you should never desist in trying again to win people.

Many of us have fished in the same waters over and over again. We have been trying to win certain members of our families for months and years. I believe Jesus would say to us; "Go back to the same waters, and throw your net out again, this time the fish are coming in, do not desist but rather persist and you will see my Word fulfilled."

A fellow minister tells the story of how he organised his church members into groups that were responsible for a block of houses in each neighbourhood. These groups would visit each home every Saturday morning offering to help or be of service. They would knock on the front door and say; "Hi, we are your neighbourhood servants. Can we help you in any way today?" At first they were met with startled looks and short answers, but through persistence (going back every Saturday) people began to open up their homes and their hearts to them. Now through the relationships they establish, countless families are being won to Christ. Their persistence is breaking down resistance. We should do the same. As someone once said: "Go the extra mile. It's never crowded!"

2ND PERSISTENCE PRINCIPLE:
Champions do what needs to be done even when they don't feel like it.

In Matthew 28 Jesus gave His last instructions to His disciples. 'Go!' he said. However, many people are still waiting to be led by the Lord or for an angel to arrive in their house with specific instructions to evangelise. We need to be careful that we do not treat the Great Commission with a great omission!

Just as the flesh does not like to pray or fast nor does it like to evangelise. It will give you a hundred other suggestions to do in the place of taking the time and effort to invite people to your cell groups and to church services.

Imagine if Christ had decided to be led of the flesh in Gethsemane! It was late, he was tired, he had just had supper, the others were sleeping, and the cup of wrath that was on offer would lead to terrible suffering, mockery and the agony of death on a cross. Yet thank God he chose to follow the call of God on his life.

His great imitator, the Apostle Paul, was persecuted, beaten, reviled, defamed and attacked (1Cor 4:11-13) but still pressed on. Wonderfully even after he had been stoned at (Acts 14:19) and left for dead, his persistence was not dampened. He resolved to go back to the very city from which he was rejected!

Commitment is to finish a task
long after the enthusiasm has worn off.

The tempter comes to us all, subtly calling us to desist in our holy pursuits. "Don't be too extreme" he says, "Be like the majority, they are sleeping and eating now. Relax! Your enthusiasm will only cause you harm."

I remember when I started my ministry I was passionately talking to some visiting friends of their need of Christ. With them was another Christian who listened to me for a while and then interrupted me and said, "It is obvious you have been recently saved. After a while your desire to win people for Christ will cool down." I replied, "With all due respect, if you think I am hot today for the cause of Christ today, I have news for you, I hope to be hotter in the future!"

3rd **PERSISTENCE** Principle:
Everybody takes knocks,
but champions are the ones who get up quickly.

"Great people are really just ordinary people with an extraordinary amount of determination. Great people don't know how to quit."

Rick Warren

There will be times in our lives when we all experience rejection, and I am sure, none of us likes the feeling. But would anything ever be achieved in life if people quit at the first sign of trouble? I spent sometime training to sell life insurance. I can't remember a day in my life having so many people close their doors to me with a firm "No, not interested!" I have memories of trudging home nursing my wounds. But, insurance companies teach their agents, for every 100 no's you will find 1 yes! It is a numbers game. Somebody out there wants what you have got. You have to simply go through the lists to find that person. As someone once said; "To become a great champion, fight one more round"

*Every boxer knows that the battle is not lost if they fall
but if they stay on the ground*

In our work as evangelists we must not take rejection personally. If people do not hear our message, we must cry out for them in our prayers and continue to sow into their lives, but, at the same time we must move on to minister to others. Sow the seed, and then move on to the next field! This is wisdom. And we can hope, as Paul did, that when they see others converting this will provoke them to jealously and lead them to convert too. (Rom 11:11).

> *"By perseverance the snail reached the ark!"*
>
> Charles Spurgeon

David Brainerd, the 18th Century missionary to the North American Red Indians, spent years toiling away before he saw his first convert. But once the wall of indifference had been pierced a revival swept through their communities.

More recently I listened to a pastor of one of the largest churches in Buenos Aires recount his story of preaching for over a thousand times in a local downtown park with very little result. But he persisted and the floodgates were opened.

> *The man who moved the mountain began*
> *by carrying away small stones.*

Do not quit when you takes knocks or set-backs. God allows these to come your way in order to reveal your true character and faithfulness to the natural and spiritual world. The Old Testament story of Job shows how pressing on in faith when afflictions come, and not slipping into to blaming God or shaming others, leads to blessings in abundance.

The Bible teaches that we need to have faith and patience in order to inherit the promises of God (Heb 6:12). It is easy to believe God for something for a short while. But if the promise does not come quickly many people quit believing. (In reality these people never really believed, for faith is to believe no matter how long the promise takes on coming. You believe it because God promised it.)

I believe in Psalm 2:8;

"Ask of me, and I shall give You the nations for Your inheritance, and the ends of the earth for Your possession."

I believe that Christ will redeem a people from every tribe, nation and tongue. Likewise I believe that "If you believe in the Lord Jesus Christ you will be saved, you and your household" (Acts 16:31). Salvation is a blessing for every member of our families.

Do not forget to add patience to your faith. Keep believing, even when the situation seems impossible. Abram believed that God would give him a son when both he and his wife Sarah were well past the child-bearing age. Have bull-dog faith. Don't let go of the promises! Press on persistently.

PENTECOST Principles

"Religion is a dish to be served hot; once it becomes lukewarm it is sickening. Our baptism must be with the Holy Ghost and with fire if we would win the masses to hear the gospel."

Charles Spurgeon

1st PENTECOST Principle:
You are empowered through a personal Pentecost.

It is well-known that the Apostle Peter denied the Lord Jesus Christ in front of a slave girl during the trial of His master. Fulfilling the prophesy, the cock crowed three times, and Peter, realising his own fickleness and fear, went away and wept bitterly. He had denied Christ, the very person he promised to stand by through thick and thin.

Yet less than two weeks later, a different Peter emerged. This Peter rose up with the eleven apostles and preached Christ with boldness and revelation to the amazed multitude. Now he confronted the people who had, some weeks before, yelled out for Christ's crucifixion (Mark 15:13-14). Then he had denied knowing Christ to a young slave girl, now he was preaching Christ to a huge crowd of religiously sensitive men.

What had happened between then and now? How had Peter changed so dramatically? Why was he no longer concerned about self but concerned about God? The answer is divinely simple and profound at the same time: Pentecost had changed his life forever.

Many of us are natural cowards when it comes to evangelism. We know we should reach out to those around us but we are afraid that that we may be disliked or rejected. A personal Pentecost is needed.

When a person is filled with the Holy Spirit he breaks out of the restraints of being self-conscious and he becomes God-conscious. He is no longer interested in serving the selfish interests of man but the noble interests of

God.

Through Pentecost, this person has touched eternity and tasted the glories of the age to come. He has glimpsed the wonders of heaven above. He has become separated to God and sanctified by God and hence useful in His hands. He now has one desire – to please His Lord and Saviour. A zeal for God's house consumes him (John 2:17). He cannot hold back for the word of God is like a fire locked up in his bones that he must release (Jer 20:9).

*One touch of God can change you
more than a thousand words.*

One touch of God can change your life forever. John Wesley's life was transformed when he felt his heart "strangely warmed" by the Holy Spirit. Smith Wigglesworth, the well-known apostle of faith and healing, was unable to speak publicly because of a serious speech impediment. But from the day he was baptised in the Spirit, a flow of revelation and anointing burst forth in his life that touched and healed thousands of lives around the globe.

I am not suggesting that we should not preach sermons. Of course not! But what I am saying is that we need to give people opportunity not just to hear the word of God but to be ministered to by the Holy Spirit. The Word is the Bread of Life. The Spirit is the Water of Life. If people just hear the word they become dry. If they just drink the Spirit they become flabby. But if we offer a balanced diet of Bread and Water, or Word and Spirit, lives will grow healthily.

And it shall come to pass in that day, that his burden will be taken away from your shoulder, and his yoke from your neck, and the yoke will be destroyed because of the anointing. (Isa 10:27)

The church is full of believers who were addicted to some vice, be it pornography, alcohol, but one touch of God has changed their lives forever. One taste of God's heavenly wine and the earth's wine begins to lose its flavour. What the world has to offer can never satisfy the soul, but Jesus promised living water that if we would drink we would never thirst again (John 4). In other words, it is the Holy Spirit that brings the satisfaction that we are all looking for.

How little chance the Holy Ghost has nowadays. The churches and missionary societies have so bound him in red tape that they practically ask Him to sit in a corner while they do the work themselves.
C.T. Studd

2ND PENTECOST PRINCIPLE:
YOUR FUNCTION IS TO FLOW IN GOD'S UNCTION.

There is no better evangelist in the world than the Holy Spirit.
D.L. Moody

When John the Baptist introduced Jesus at the river Jordan he explained:

"I indeed baptise you with water unto repentance: but He who is coming after me is mightier than I, whose sandals I am not worthy to carry, He will baptise you with the Holy Spirit and with fire" (Mt 3:11)

The anointing of the Holy Spirit brings power to what we say and how we say it. As we speak the Lord brings revelations to us to enable us to minister directly in the hearts of others.

Modern communication techniques, creativity and charisma have their place in connecting with today's generation. However, they are to no avail if not backed up by the anointing. An anointed voice always gains attention and silences a crowd, whether it is spoken through a microphone or not. It is the life force of Christ flowing through us that counts.

The Word of God in an unanointed mouth is weak and pathetic but in the mouth of an anointed minister it becomes like a hammer that is able to break the hardest stone – the hardest heart (Jer 23:29). Ministers who speak with Holy Ghost fire convict their hearers immediately; arguments are smashed, lies destroyed, truth is revealed.

Anointed preaching often produces a mixed response. When Jesus preached people either wanted to leave everything and follow Him or throw Him off a mountain top! The Apostle Steven preached with such fire that the leaders of the Jews covered their ears, and then later stoned him to death. However, the disciples made "great lamentation" over his death and carried him off for an honourable burial (Acts 6:57-58, Acts 7:2). Similarly the Apostle Paul preach with such conviction to King Agrippa and Governor Festus that the latter cried out "Paul, you are beside yourself, much learning has made you mad!" (Acts 26:14). However, he won many others to Christ who were in the king's service.

Thankfully in most western countries, where freedom of speech is permitted, it is against the law for people to respond violently when they don't agree. But even so the crowd still tend to divide when the fire of God falls. You will find some people love it and others hate it. Why? – Because the Spirit of God reveals what is in hidden in their hearts. When the light of the Gospel shines forth, some people run into the light grateful to know the true way to Life, but others, retreat into darkness unless their evil ways are exposed. If you turn a light on a night in the cellar, some insects come to the light, but cockroaches always flee!

Then the Spirit of the Lord will come upon you, and you will prophesy with them and be turned into another man (1 Sam 10:6).

Holy fire is available today in order to enable us to minister effectively. When the anointing is upon a preacher, dramatic changes can be seen in their manner and posture. I have seen quite reserved individuals transformed in an instant into passionate preachers filled with wisdom and revelation of heaven. They light up with the fire of God and the ambience of the meeting changes completely. Many times, when I have stood up to minister, it has felt as if I am standing on top of a huge gas cooker that is blasting its flames up from under my feet.

Any method of evangelism will work if God is in it.
Leonard Ravenhill

Crowds in their thousands flooded to hear 18th Century preacher John Wesley at a time when sin was rife and religion was dead in England. The country was steeped in prostitution and alcoholism (with the advent of the drink Gin). At the time someone asked him why so many people would come to hear him speak and he simply answered: "I set myself on fire and people come to watch me burn!"

On the day of Pentecost the fire fell, the disciples were transformed and the net result was that three thousand were saved and added to the church. If the fire of the Spirit made the difference to their ministries, then we need our own personal Pentecost if we are to have the same results as the early church. If God sent the fire to help those who had walked personally with Christ, how much more do we, who live 2000 years later, need it in our ministries?

If you preach the word with boldness,
God will confirm it with signs.

In my early ministry I travelled from island to island in the Philippines holding evangelistic rallies in town squares and basketball courts. I was usually nervous when we arrived in each island to see how the locals would take to us. I had seen God's Spirit move powerfully to save, heal and baptise in other places, but I was anxious to know if He would move again here. Finally the Lord opened my eyes to the truth as I read the following passage:

So then, after the Lord had spoken to them, He was received up into heaven, and sat down at the right hand of God. And they went out and **preached everywhere, the Lord working with them and confirming** the word through the accompanying signs.
Amen. (Mark 16:19-20, emphasis mine)

The disciples did the preaching, God did the confirming. I realised in an instant that if I am faithful to preach the word, God is faithful to confirm it with signs following. As I declared the truth, He would send the power. When a preacher becomes unashamed about Gospel truth, the power of God to save is released (Rom 1:16).

> *God's part is to put forth power; our part is to put forth faith.*
>
> Andrew A. Bonar

This understanding released me to a new level of faith. I also realised that, whilst verse 19 stated that the Lord sat down at God's right hand in heaven, verse 20 states that the Lord was still working with them to confirm their words. Friends, we never minister alone. Christ is with us, in the form of the Holy Spirit. As we speak in His name, His Spirit is commissioned to glorify it.

When Jesus taught the Word, the power of God became present to heal people (Luke 5:17). When we teach the same power is available. What is needed is for each of us to be baptised in the Holy Spirit and fire and, from then on, to believe that in the "greater One" who lives within us (1John 4:4). For nothing is too difficult for the Lord (Mark 10:27).

Jesus started his earthly ministry after the Holy Spirit came upon Him by the river Jordan. The disciples started their ministries after the Holy Spirit filled them in the upper-room on the day of Pentecost. We must have our own personal baptism of fire. Given the same equipment we will see similar results.

3rd PENTECOST Principle:
YOU CAN ONLY GIVE WHAT YOU HAVE RECEIVED.

> *Oh for a passionate passion for souls.*
> *Oh for a pity that yearns!*
> *Oh for the love that loves unto death,*
> *Oh for the fire that burns!*
> *Oh for the pure prayer-power that prevails,*
> *that pours itself out for the lost.*
> *Victorious prayer in the Conqueror's Name,*
> *Oh for a Pentecost!*
>
> Amy Carmichael

It is one thing to have a desire to win your world. It is another thing to have the equipment to do that. Every worker needs to be adequately equipped in order to complete the assigned task. Many an army has been defeated due to soldiers not having adequate weaponry or ammunition. Similarly too many ministers burn up or quietly fade away because they tried to do things without the endowment of the Holy Spirit.

Jesus told His disciples that they would become His witness after the Holy Spirit had come upon them (Acts 1:8). Until then they could not be true representatives of the risen Christ. But after they had received the power they would be able to minister with power.

Your spiritual impact is never larger than your own spiritual temperature. The miracle through you will never be larger than the miracle in you. There is a time to give but there is also a time to receive from God. If you want to change the world you must first change your world.

> *There has never been a great awakening of sinners*
> *until there has first been a great revival*
> *in the heart of a minister.*

Acts chapter three narrates the account of Peter and John going to the temple to pray at the appointed hour. As they pass the Gate called Beautiful a beggar cries out to them for alms. Peter's response is revealing:

Then Peter said, "Silver and gold I do not have, but what I do have I give you: in the name of Jesus Christ of Nazareth, rise up and walk". (Acts 3:6)

This man leaped to his feet and began praising God. No doubt Peter and John had passed him many other times. Perhaps they had given offerings to him on previous occasions such as the Law commanded that they do. But today was different; they had something different to give. Yesterday they did not have it, but today they did. Listen to Peter's words: "What I do have I give you". Peter had something to give in the form of the power of the Holy Spirit and he was willing to give that freely.

What have you received from God? Let him do a deep work in your life. Let Him fill you up until you are running over with His presence. King David exclaimed in Psalm 23: "You anoint my head with oil and my cup runs over". No wonder he was such a formidable king and leader. The power of God was upon him. In all our getting, we must get the power promised through a personal Pentecost. Once the Spirit breaks out from within you, you will find rivers will flow from your innermost being that will never run dry (John 7:37-38).

In the last chapter we spoke about passion. Whilst passion attracts it cannot be imitated for long. If it is only an imitation it will fizzle out sooner or later. But if you are baptised in the Holy Spirit, you will have a fountain of passion bubbling up on the inside of you each and every day.

When we are saved we draw living water out of the wells of salvation (Isa 12:3). When we are baptised in the Spirit rivers of water begin to flow from our hearts (John 7:38).

It is important not to fall into the erroneous thinking that once you are baptised in the Spirit you do not need to have new times of empowering. Occasionally I met a brother or sister in Christ who tell me that they were baptised in the Spirit twenty or thirty years ago and yet they seem to be so dry now. What is the problem here? They believed that the infilling of the Spirit is a one-time affair. A paradox exists in that we receive the Spirit when we confess our faith in Christ, yet we can always be receiving more of him.

Do not be drunk with wine, in which is dissipation, but be filled with the Spirit, speaking to one another in psalms and hymns and spiritual songs, singing and making melody in your heart to the Lord. (Eph 5:18-19)

Paul wrote this letter to believers at Ephesus who had already been baptised in the Spirit. He was not encouraging them to have this experience for the first time but, like those who drink wine, to be regularly drinking the anointing in order to effectively minister to God and to people. The literal translation of the phrase "be filled" is a present continuous verb in the Greek testament – "Be you being filled by the Holy Spirit".

Acts Chapter four accounts the arrest of Peter and John and their subsequent release after a series of serious threats from the Pharisees and scribes not to preach in the name of Jesus Christ. The apostles return to their brothers and joined together to pray. They implored God to stretch out his hand to perform mighty wonders to demonstrate that Jesus is the Christ. In response to prayer the Bible states:

And when they had prayed, the place where they were assembled together was shaken; and **they were all filled with the Holy Spirit**, and they spoke the word of God with boldness. (Acts 4:31, emphasis mine)

In Acts Chapter Two the disciples were shaken and filled by the power of the Holy Spirit; in Acts Chapter Four the whole building is shaken by the power of the Holy Spirit. For the apostles this was a type of second baptism - a greater baptism. "With great power the apostles gave witness to the resurrection of the Lord Jesus" (Acts 4:33). If the disciples were in need of further infillings, I believe you and I are. The anointing prepares us for the task at hand.

King David said; "I have been anointed with fresh oil" (Psalm 92:10). Every car needs to change its oil after a certain distance. In similar fashion a Christian needs fresh oil in order to maintain a living relationship with the Lord and have fresh fire to minister to the people.

God pours out His Spirit upon His children for a purpose. It is not just to make us feel good. Jesus said: "The Spirit of the Lord is upon Me, because He has anointed me to preach the Gospel to the poor…" (Luke 4:18). Equipped with His power we are able to conquer our generation for Christ. His promises become attainable, not because of our talent, charisma, our merit, but because of the supernatural power of the Spirit with in us. Jesus said:
"He who believes in Me, the works that I do he will do also; and greater works than these will he do, because I go to My Father… and I will pray the

Father, and He will give you another Helper, that He may abide with you forever - the Spirit of truth" (John 14:12-17)

Dear friends, great men and women of God have gone before us. Like Jesus they were anointed by God "with the Holy Ghost and power, and went about doing good and healing all those who were oppressed of the devil" (Acts 10:38). These men and women of former generations have been and gone, passing the holy mantle to us. They have left but the same Holy Spirit remains. The anointing that was on Jesus is here today. The anointing, that equipped Peter and Paul and the other apostles, is here today. The anointing that burned like fire in the hearts of the men and women who shaped church history is available for us today.

The power of Pentecost is the fuel behind these High Productivity Principles. If you are filled with the Spirit you will be compelled to fulfil the other principles mentioned in this book. You will be inclined to pay the price, to pray, to prioritise, to prepare yourself, to partner together, to provide, to keep the right perspective, to be passionate and persistent.

So seek fresh power from on high. Go to the Lord in prayer, as the disciples did in Acts Chapter Two. Ask Him to fill you right now. Jesus taught us how to receive heavenly power:

If you being evil give good gifts to your children, so much more will the heavenly Father give the Holy Spirit to those who ask Him. (Luke 10.12)

The Lord is telling us that the Holy Spirit is a present, or in other words, this baptism of fire is a present. He does not give it to us because we deserve it or have earned. He does not give it to us because we are holy but rather in order to make us holy. He gives it freely because he is a giving God. Jesus contrasts earthly parents with His heavenly Father. If unregenerate selfish earthly fathers give presents to their children, imagine how much more the giving generous gracious heavenly Father wants to give to His children. Men might buy gifts of toys and clothes and other material blessings, but the heavenly Father gives His very own Spirit. With His Spirit comes His power.

The only thing that you need to do to receive this power is to ask in faith and then act in faith. So ask the Lord right now. He is waiting to respond. Ask Him to open up a fountain of rivers inside of you that will flow out of you. Ask Him to baptise you with a new heavenly language. New words are to flow out of your spirit as His Spirit flows into yours. It is an angelic language. It is a heavenly language. It is deep calling out to deep. It is a love language; no longer limited by the restrictions of human vocabulary but free to flow and to express its deepest innermost thoughts and feeling to the Great Spirit on High.

Permit this power to flow through you and, as you practice the principles, you will become a fruitful witness and a father or mother to many spiritual children. Practice these principles at home, in your cell groups, in your church and you will boost your productivity. Friends the harvest is ripe. Let us sharpen our sickles, or better still, let us service our combine harvesters, and get to work. Thousands on earth are waiting for us to arrive. Thousands in heaven are cheering us on.

Those who sow in tears shall reap in joy. He who continually goes forth weeping, bearing seed for sowing, shall doubtless come again with rejoicing, bringing his sheaves with him. (Ps 126:5-6)

Conclusion

Finally do remember that it is by practising the principles that you will see the results. It is not enough to read a recipe book to become a fine chef - you need to get the pots out and start cooking! Likewise it is not enough to be merely a "hearer of the word" – you need to be a "doer" if you want to produce much fruit. Put the principles into practice and you will rejoice in the results.

Friends, now that you have read this book please fall down upon your knees and ask God to fill you with His Spirit as He did to the disciples in the Book of Acts. I believe the power of God will fall on you as you act in faith. God wants to equip you now for the incredible ministry He has for you.

Appendix

Information about The 11th Question Project
The spiritual self-evaluation test

How was the 11th Question Project born?

In May 2007, whilst my wife and I were based with Videira Church in Goiania, Brazil, we had the pleasure of hosting German Evangelist Reinhard Bonnke and the Christ for All Nations team. He told of us his goal of winning 100 million souls for Christ in 10 years and of the extraordinary results they are seeing in Africa and beyond.

On his departure I entered into a sort of spiritual crisis. We had been seeing wonderful results in our Gospel campaigns, the churches in our network were growing steadily and healthily. But we dreamed of winning so many more. (Evangelists don't count the number of people in the church, but the number of people still on the outside!) I reasoned that if we had the same Bible and the same Holy Spirit as brother Bonnke, then our vision for winning souls was too small.

One afternoon I was lying on my bed, thinking about the millions of unsaved in our world, and I sensed the Lord speak to me. No angel entered my room (I have only seen one angel in my life, and that one I married!). No audible voice, but rather, a question slipped quietly yet forcibly into my heart and seemed to echo there. I can still hear it today; "Giles, what would you do, if I asked you to win 100 million souls in the next 10 years?"

Friends, to cut a story short, I resolved to do two things. I wrote two books – one for believers, the other for unbelievers. Firstly I wanted to inspire and instruct other believers on how to boost their evangelistic productivity. That's how this book that you are now reading came about and I pray your results will forever be changed because of applying these principles. The second book I wrote is entirely for unbelievers.

If you go to a Christian bookstore you will find thousands of books written for the edification of believers, but hardly even one written for the Lost. In my opinion this is a huge disequilibrium. The church is called to be "Light to the World" and "Salt to the earth" but we have so little written for unbelievers. Hence I wrote The 11th Question – The Spiritual Self-Evaluation Test. (I explain the rational and the content of the book below.)

What happened next was extraordinary - over 100,000 people read the book and did the test in the first month of its launch. Churches all around Brazil began to launch outreach campaigns using the 11Q Test material. Almost everyday I hear reports of conversions, new cell groups starting, and churches growing as a result. By God's grace I believe we have designed a manner of sharing the glorious Gospel in a cringe-free, yet cutting-edge manner. For this reason, thousands of believers are buying the books in quantity to use with their friends and family members.

I believe a number of reasons have helped it be so user-friendly:
1. There are people who don't like to listen to sermons but who are open to do a self-evaluation test.
2. The booklet is full of little stories and modern parables which help believers break the ice and explain the hidden truths of the Gospel. (Jesus used many stories to communicate and I know that we preachers love to use stories too).
3. It is short, easy to read, and full of cartoon illustrations to help those who are not accustomed to read.
4. It is very focussed and deals purely with leading the reader to genuine conviction and then genuine conversion. There are other reasons why the 11Q Project is seeing such great results.

In the following pages I have given a fuller explanation. I believe that it will enable you to win thousands for Christ in your own city.

What is the rational behind the test? The major evangelistic challenge that we face today is the fact that our generation is influenced by humanistic teachings that state that Man is good. Because of this many people do not realise that they are spiritually dead and therefore do not value what Christ did for them.

Our test has 11 questions. The first ten questions are based on the 10 commandments. In Galatians 3:24, the Apostle Paul wrote: The Law is our school-master that brings us to Christ. Likewise in 1Timothy 1:8-11, Paul teaches that the Law is not for the Just but for sinners. In Romans chapter 7:7, he explains that without the law he would not have known sin.

The Law reveals sin, which is the heart of the human problem. It allows us to do a true and inner diagnosis and discover the root of human selfishness and of worldwide death and destruction. The Law or the Commandments reveal our true spiritual condition and consequential condemnation and thereby awakens us to the need of a Saviour.

We all have friends and relations who have not expressed an interest in Jesus - this maybe because of the way that we have presented the Gospel. All Christians believe that Jesus is the remedy to the world's problems or, in other words, He is the medicine of the world. However, very few people like to take medicine! That is until they understand that they are sick or dying. Many of us have tried to offer the medicine of Christ to friends, without first showing that they are sick. Therefore few have accepted.

People only appreciate the work of Christ on the cross until they realise their own eternal destiny. 19th Century preacher Charles Spurgeon said; "The message of mercy makes no sense outside the context of judgment". There can be no genuine conversion if there is no genuine conviction.

The 11th Question Test does not condemn people (we are already condemned), but rather wakes them up to their real condition. It this point it announces the best news ever heard by the world – that despite our sins and transgressions, God loves us and has made a way out of castigation and condemnation into new life for everyone who believes. The 11th Question is the most important question in the world – Do you want to receive Jesus as Lord and Saviour?

Outline of the Book:

1. Introduction

After an ice-breaker story the book starts by showing that tests are good for us because they reveal reality. We mention that there are many tests in life; this test is to reveal your spiritual condition. The first 10 questions are based on the 10 Commandments. Interestingly the Commandments are valued by all the major religions, all Christian denominations and are the basis of legal systems in all developed nations.

2. The 10 Questions

Each page of the book details one of the commandments, a story with an illustration, an explanation and the question: Have you always kept this commandment? Yes or No

3. Results and Consequences

The reader must evaluate his or her answers, after which we explain that there is a consequence to breaking God's law. The scripture teaches that the wages of sin is death.

4. The Solution

We reveal that God is both just and merciful – even though we deserve to die He does not wants us to. Therefore He sent His son to die in our place. The end of the book is the 11th QUESTION: Do you want to receive Jesus as your Saviour and Lord? Yes or No.

5. The Invitations

The final page of the booklet gives space for believers to write church information and, in particular, to put 3 invitations:

   a) Invitation to cell group / home group
   b) Invitation to Church Service
   c) Invitation to Harvest Event / Crusade

How does the Campaign work?

The 11th Question book was written to be a tool to communicate the Gospel through a test. The purpose is to mobilise every member of your church and thereby release the potential to win many people for Christ.

In each city we recommend the following strategy to obtain the greatest results:

1. Launch Weekend

The campaign starts with a weekend of training and revival. The goal is to:

> a) Teach your members the Principles of Effective Evangelism based on this book Winning Your World.
> b) Train your members to use the booklet *The 11th Question – the spiritual self-evaluation test.*
> c) Minister to everyone so that each member has a personal Pentecost and receives the fire and passion to evangelise the city.

2. Campaign

Whilst the test can be applied at anytime we recommend that you launch an intensive campaign that lasts between 21 to 40 days in order to gain maximum results.

There are many ways by which the test can be applied:

Every Member:
> The goal is for each member to do at least 20 tests during the campaign (some believers will do more, some will do less). Each member will receive a card on which he will write the names of 5 friends, 5 relations, 5 neighbours and 5 unknowns. With this card the member can focus their efforts and pastors can monitor progress. In this way a church of 200 has the potential of reaching 4000 people; a church of 1000 can reach 20,000. When churches work together they can literally challenge the whole city to do the test.

Cell Groups:
: The test can be presented by multi-media power-point for guest meetings and dinner parties organised by the cell group.

Schools:
: On invitation teams can present the test in schools, class by class.

Businesses:
: As above, in break-times the 11th Q Test can be applied to employees, through multi-media presentation or using the booklets.

Radio:
: A live test can be done on the radio with the listeners invited to a follow-up meeting afterwards.

Guest Services:
: Each Sunday invite your guests to a special reception that takes place during the Sunday sermon in a separate venue. Guests are greeted cordially and, as a way to help them understand why we believe in Christ, the 11th Q test is presented to them. At the end of the service the guests are ushered back into the church service and received with applause by the local congregation.

3. HARVEST EVENT

The campaign ends with a large harvest event/crusade where the 11th Question is presented publicly and appeals are made for those to receive Christ as Saviour and for healing and the baptism of the Holy Spirit. We also recommend that new converts receive a free copy of the 11th Question booklet so that he or she is immediately equipped to do the test with their own family and friends.

OTHER INFORMATION

1. PRAYER CAMPAIGN

We recommend that you launch an extended campaign of prayer and fasting either before or during the evangelistic campaign. In our experience most believers are able to commit to a fast of one meal per day for 3 weeks or more and to participate in prayer meetings during the week.

2. ADVERTISING CAMPAIGN

It is also a good idea to awaken interest in your community for the project through an advertising campaign. Consider issuing each church member with a T-shirt and badge that says, "Have you answered the 11th Question? Ask me what it is." Likewise effective campaigns can be held in through the radio and television and through pamphlet distribution and billboards. The advertisements should include telephone numbers to follow-up.

3. PARTICIPATION

The 11th Question will work for small churches and large churches alike. We would encourage church leaders to invite all Bible-based churches in their cities to do the project jointly so that whole cities can be challenged to do the test. Experience shows that local churches win more converts when working together on evangelistic projects.

Other books by Giles Stevens:

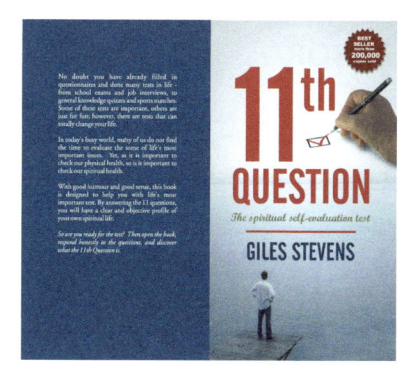

The 11th Question – the spiritual self-evaluation test.

The best-selling outreach tool that helps believers share their faith with friends and families through a self-evaluation test. The premise of this book is that people only drink medicine (material or spiritual) when they first know that they are sick. For use in evangelistic campaigns or give out as a present to your friends.

Church leaders – if you would like a DVD that shows how to launch a campaign in your community, please contact our office.

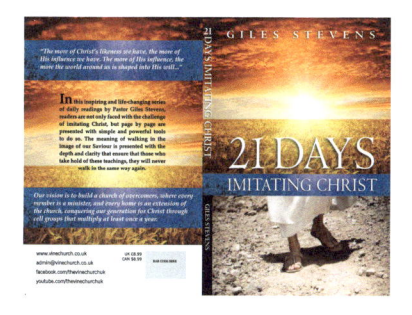

21 Days imitating Christ

In this inspiring and life-changing series of daily readings by Pastor Giles Stevens, readers are not only faced with the challenge of imitating Christ, but page by page are presented with simply and powerful tools to do so. The meaning of walking in the image of our Saviour is presented with a depth and clarity that ensure that, for those who take hold of these teachings, they will never walk in the same way again.

For more information & materials, please contact us:

The Vine Studio, 5 Blackworth Court, Highworth, SN6 7NS
Tel: 01793 862 224
www.vinechurch.co.uk
admin@vinechurch.co.uk

About the Author

Giles Stevens and his wife Silvia pastor Vine Church UK – an international cell church based in the city of Swindon, UK. Previously he worked as an evangelist in Asia and South America.

The broader network, Vine Church International, is becoming known worldwide as a place where "every member is a minister" and for its vision of building churches of "overcomers".

Giles' first book "The 11th Question – the spiritual self-analysis test" became an instant best seller. Other books now include; Winning Your World, 21 days to Refresh Your Relationships, & Joshua's Journey.

Contact: admin@vinechurch.co.uk
Tel: 01793 862224